endorsed for
::BTEC

REVISE BTEC NATIONAL
Sport
UNITS 1 AND

D0351866

REVIS   OK

Series Consultant: H

Authors: Sue Hartig

While the publishers have made
qualification and its assessmen
assessment guidance materials
and should always be referred

This qualification is reviewed o
Any such updates that affect t
at www.pearsonfe.co.uk/BTEC

A note from the pul

In order to ensure that this res   o any sections
support for the associated Pear   apers for which
been through a review process
This process confirms that this resource fully covers   Examiners will not use endorsed resources as a source
the teaching and learning content of the specification   of material for any assessment set by Pearson.
or part of a specification at which it is aimed. It also
confirms that it demonstrates an appropriate balance   Endorsement of a resource does not mean that the
between the development of subject skills, knowledge   resource is required to achieve this Pearson qualification,
and understanding, in addition to preparation for   nor does it mean that it is the only suitable material
assessment.   available to support the qualification, and any resource
                                                             lists produced by the awarding body shall include this
Endorsement does not cover any guidance on   and other appropriate resources.
assessment activities or processes (e.g. practice
questions or advice on how to answer assessment
questions), included in the resource nor does it
prescribe any particular approach to the teaching or
delivery of a related course.

**For the full range of Pearson revision titles across KS2,
KS3, GCSE, Functional Skills, AS/A Level and BTEC visit:**
www.pearsonschools.co.uk/revise

P Pearson

Published by Pearson Education Limited, 80 Strand, London, WC2R 0RL.

www.pearsonschoolsandfecolleges.co.uk

Copies of official specifications for all Pearson qualifications may be found on the website:
qualifications.pearson.com
Text and illustrations © Pearson Education 2017
Typeset and illustrated by Kamae Design
Produced by Out of House Publishing
Cover illustration by Miriam Sturdee

The rights of Sue Hartigan and Kelly Sharp to be identified as authors of this work have been
asserted by them in accordance with the Copyright, Designs and Patents Act 1988.

First published 2017

20 19 18 17
10 9 8 7 6 5 4 3 2 1

British Library Cataloguing in Publication Data
A catalogue record for this book is available from the British Library

ISBN 978 1 292 23060 3

Printed in Italy by Lego S.p.A

Acknowledgements
The publisher would like to thank the following for their kind permission to reproduce their
photographs:

Getty Images: Alexander Nemenov / AFP 19, Charles Bertram / Lexington Herald-Leader / TNS 20,
Mark Ralston / AFP 17; **Shutterstock.com:** Bojan656 6, John Kershner 9, Mitch Gunn 3

All other images © Pearson Education

Notes from the publisher
1. In order to ensure that this resource offers high-quality support for the associated Pearson qualification, it
has been through a review process by the awarding body. This process confirms that this resource fully covers
the teaching and learning content of the specification or part of a specification at which it is aimed. It also
confirms that it demonstrates an appropriate balance between the development of subject skills, knowledge
and understanding, in addition to preparation for assessment.

Endorsement does not cover any guidance on assessment activities or processes (e.g. practice questions or
advice on how to answer assessment questions), included in the resource nor does it prescribe any particular
approach to the teaching or delivery of a related course.

While the publishers have made every attempt to ensure that advice on the qualification and its assessment is
accurate, the official specification and associated assessment guidance materials are the only authoritative source
of information and should always be referred to for definitive guidance.

Pearson examiners have not contributed to any sections in this resource relevant to examination papers for
which they have responsibility.

Examiners will not use endorsed resources as a source of material for any assessment set by Pearson.

Endorsement of a resource does not mean that the resource is required to achieve this Pearson qualification,
nor does it mean that it is the only suitable material available to support the qualification, and any resource lists
produced by the awarding body shall include this and other appropriate resources.

2. Pearson has robust editorial processes, including answer and fact checks, to ensure the accuracy of the
content in this publication, and every effort is made to ensure this publication is free of errors. We are, however,
only human, and occasionally errors do occur. Pearson is not liable for any misunderstandings that arise as a
result of errors in this publication, but it is our priority to ensure that the content is accurate. If you spot an error,
please do contact us at resourcescorrections@pearson.com so we can make sure it is corrected.

Websites

Pearson Education Limited is not responsible for the content of any external internet sites. It is essential for
tutors to preview each website before using it in class so as to ensure that the URL is still accurate, relevant and
appropriate. We suggest that tutors bookmark useful websites and consider enabling students to access them
through the school/college intranet.

Introduction

This Workbook has been designed to help you revise the skills you may need for the externally assessed units of your course. Remember that you won't necessarily be studying all the units included here – it will depend on the qualification you are taking.

BTEC National Qualification	Externally assessed units
Certificate	1 Anatomy and Physiology
Extended Certificate	1 Anatomy and Physiology 2 Fitness Training and Programming for Health, Sport and Well-being
Foundation Diploma	1 Anatomy and Physiology 2 Fitness Training and Programming for Health, Sport and Well-being
Diploma (Fitness Services)	1 Anatomy and Physiology 2 Fitness Training and Programming for Health, Sport and Well-being

Your Workbook

Each unit in this Workbook contains either one or two sets of revision questions or revision tasks, to help you **revise the skills** you may need in your assessment. The selected content, outcomes, questions and answers used in each unit are provided to help you to revise content and ways of applying your skills. Ask your tutor or check the Pearson website for the most up-to-date **Sample Assessment Material** and **Mark Schemes** to get an indication of the structure of your actual assessment and what this requires of you. The detail of the actual assessment may change so always make sure you are up to date.

This Workbook will often include one or more useful features that explain or break down longer questions or tasks. Remember that these features won't appear in your actual assessment!

> Grey boxes like this contain **hints and tips** about ways that you might complete a task, interpret a brief, understand a concept or structure your responses.

 This icon will appear next to an **example partial answer** to a revision question or task. You should read the partial answer carefully, then complete it in your own words.

> This is a revision activity. It will help you understand some of the skills needed to complete the revision task or question..

> 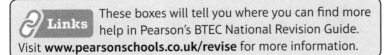 These boxes will tell you where you can find more help in Pearson's BTEC National Revision Guide.

Visit **www.pearsonschools.co.uk/revise** for more information.

There is often space on the pages for you to write in. However, if you are making ongoing notes you may want to use a separate piece of paper. Similarly, some units will be assessed through submission of digital files, or on screen, rather than on paper. Ask your tutor or check the Pearson website for the most up-to-date details.

Contents

Unit 1: Anatomy and Physiology

Unit 2: Fitness Training and Programming for Health, Sport and Well-being

A small bit of small print

Pearson publishes Sample Assessment Material and the Specification on its website. This is the official content and this book should be used in conjunction with it. The questions in this book have been written to help you practise the knowledge and skills you will require for your assessment. Remember: the real assessment may not look like this.

Unit 1: Anatomy and Physiology

Your exam

Unit 1 will be assessed through an exam, which will be set by Pearson. You will need to use your understanding of how the skeletal, muscular, cardiovascular and respiratory systems function and the fundamentals of the energy systems. You then respond to questions that require short and long answers.

Your Revision Workbook

> This Workbook is designed to **revise skills** that might be needed in your exam. The details of your actual exam may change from year to year so always make sure you are up to date. Ask your tutor or check the **Pearson website** for the most up-to-date **Sample Assessment Material** to get an idea of the structure of your exam and what this requires of you.

To support your revision, this Workbook contains revision questions to help you revise the skills that might be needed in your exam. These revision questions are divided into six sections.

Questions

Your response to the questions will help you to revise:
- The function of the skeletal system for sports performance (pages 1–3 and 16–17)
- The function of the muscular system for sports performance (pages 4–6 and 18–20)
- The function of the respiratory system for sports performance (pages 7–9 and 21–22)
- The function of the cardiovascular system for sports performance (pages 10–12 and 23–25)
- Energy systems for sports performance (pages 13–14 and 26–28)
- The interrelationships between body systems for sports performance, by bringing together knowledge from all the content areas (pages 15 and 29)

> **Links** To help you revise skills that might be needed in your exam this Workbook contains two sets of revision questions starting on pages 2 and 16. The first is guided and models good techniques, to help you develop your skills. The second offers less guidance as you apply your skills. See the introduction on page iii for more information on features included to help you revise.

Revision test 1

This Workbook is designed to revise the skills that might be needed in your exam. The details of the actual exam may change so always make sure you are up to date. Ask your tutor or check the Pearson website for the most up-to-date Sample Assessment Material to get an idea of the structure of the exam and what this requires of you.

Section A: Skeletal system for sports performance

Answer ALL questions. Write your answers in the spaces provided.

1 During a school ski trip a student fell and fractured his cranium.

(a) State the name of the cranium's bone type.

`1 mark`

....

....

Guided (b) Explain how the function of this bone type would help the student when he fell.

`3 marks`

Its function is to provide protection. It achieves this by

forming a ....

....

| Think about what is encased by the cranium. What is it protecting? What injury is the cranium reducing the risk of if the student fell and hit their head? |

....

....

....

....

....

Total for Question 1 = 4 marks

Guided **2** Exercise stimulates an increase of mineral uptake in the bones.

Explain the impact of this if exercise is carried out on a regular basis.

`2 marks`

Regular exercise will cause the body to adapt. The regular

increase in mineral uptake will increase the strength of the

bone, therefore reducing the risk of ....

| The question is asking for an explanation, so you should try to justify or give a reason for your answer. |

....

Total for Question 2 = 2 marks

Guided 3 | The picture shows a cricketer bowling a ball.

Analyse how the structure and function of the shoulder joint allow the cricketer to bowl the ball well.

6 marks

For an essay-style question, it is a good idea to produce a quick plan before starting to write your response. Use this plan to attempt the question.

Plan:

Type of joint – ball and socket

Structure – bones articulating to form joint

Shape/structure linked to range of movement – full range of movement

Function – bone type – leverage, red blood cell production, protection

Links to performance of technique – movements required, problems if unable to use this range of movement

Links For information on the structure and function of joints look at page 7 of the Revision Guide.

The shoulder joint is a ball and socket joint. The joint is formed by the meeting of the humerus

and scapula. The humerus forms the 'ball' in the joint, allowing the bone to ....

....

....

....

....

....

....

....

....

....

Total for Question 3 = 6 marks

TOTAL FOR SECTION A = 12 MARKS

Section B: Muscular system for sports performance

Answer ALL questions. Write your answers in the spaces provided.

Guided **4** | The body has three different muscle types. Each type is essential to successful performance in sport or exercise.

Explain **two** characteristics of cardiac muscle that make it ideal for its function. `4 marks`

> The use of **bold** in this question emphasises the word. Make sure you use this information when answering the question. Here, the word in bold emphasises that you need to explain **two** characteristics.

Two characteristics of cardiac muscle are:

1. It is non-fatiguing muscle. This makes it ideal for its function, as ....

....

....

2. It is an .... muscle. This means we do not

have to consciously think to make the heart beat, so we can concentrate on other things such as

tactics or how to perform a technique.

Total for Question 4 = 4 marks

Guided **5** | During physical activity muscles work together as antagonistic pairs.

Describe the antagonistic muscle pair action during hip flexion. `2 marks`

The hip flexors work as the agonist muscle in this movement,

as they contract ....

....

> Note how the question identifies the specific movement you need to refer to. Make sure you talk about **hip flexion**.

....

Total for Question 5 = 2 marks

Guided **6** Table 1 shows results of the vertical jump test for four different athletes.

Athlete	Rating in vertical jump test
1	Average
2	Excellent
3	Poor
4	Very good

Using these data, explain **two** physiological reasons, linked to the muscular system, why Athlete 2 achieved a higher rating than the other athletes.

4 marks

Make sure you read the questions carefully. Your answer to this question must focus on the **muscular system**. You also need to give two reasons why **Athlete 2** is better, so make sure you talk about her rather than the other athletes.

Athlete 2 may have a higher percentage of ....

muscle fibres. Therefore, she could generate more ....

allowing her to jump higher.

In addition, this athlete may have carried out more ....

....

....

....

....

Total for Question 6 = 4 marks

7 Sam uses weight training to increase her muscular strength. During a weight training session Sam's muscles contract in different ways.

Analyse how the different types of muscle contraction allow Sam to move from standing to the squat position shown, and then back to standing.

6 marks

This question asks for an **analysis**. You will need to **break down** the movement. Think about the types of muscle contraction in the different phases of the movement. Focus on the legs, as these are responsible for movement in the question context.

Plan:

Different types of muscle contraction – focus on muscle action of legs

Analysis of movement – downward phase; end of squat/stationary; upward phase

Downward phase – need to control movement against gravity

Moment when no movement but muscles still working

Movement again as move from squat to standing position

....

....

....

....

....

....

....

....

....

....

....

....

Total for Question 7 = 6 marks

TOTAL FOR SECTION B = 16 MARKS

Section C: The respiratory system for sports performance

Answer ALL questions. Write your answers in the spaces provided.

---

8 Heather is a 1500 m runner. She completes a number of fitness tests, including a treadmill test, to measure her lung volumes at rest and during exercise.

The graph shows one set of readings of Heather's lung volumes.

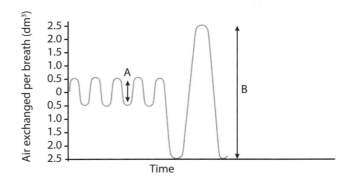

(a) Identify the lung volumes A and B.   `2 marks`

....

....

> **Guided**

(b) Explain whether the lung volumes shown in the graph are taken when Heather is resting or when she is running at varying intensities on the treadmill.   `3 marks`

The trace for tidal volume is very even. This would suggest

....

....

because ....

....

....

> Note the reference in the question to running at **varying intensities**. What happens to your breathing rate when you change from jogging to a faster pace? How would this change be reflected on a graph?

Total for Question 8 = 5 marks

9 (a) State the role of the chemoreceptors during exercise.   2 marks

....

....

....

....

> Note that **two** marks are available for this question. Try to think of two examples of the role.

Guided (b) Describe the role of the medulla oblongata in controlling breathing rate during exercise sessions of varying intensities.   3 marks

The medulla oblongata ....

....

By varying the speed of the impulses from the medulla oblongata to

the ....

....

....

> This question asks for a **description**. This means you need to **give an account of the process** to control breathing rate. However, you **do not** need to justify or give reasons in your answer.

Total for Question 9 = 5 marks

Guided

10 The Tour de France is a long-distance cycle race. Cyclists ride for 21 days and cover in excess of 3000 km, covering a variety of terrains, some at high altitude.

Assess the effect on performance of working at high altitude in a long-distance cycle race. **6 marks**

Although only a short question, lots of key information has been given. Here, **assess** means you need to **make a judgement**, possibly as a conclusion to your response. You need to explain what is significant about 'working at high altitude'. How might a difference in the partial pressure of oxygen impact on performers, in particular, 'long-distance cyclists'?

Links See page 43 of the Revision Guide for further guidance on how to approach long-answer questions.

....

....

....

....

....

....

....

....

....

....

To conclude, owing to the lower partial pressure of oxygen at altitude, and the cyclists' increased need for oxygen transport due to the intensity of the exercise they are performing, working at high altitude will make it harder for them to maintain the quality of their performance. Therefore,

they will not be able to cycle ....

....

Total for Question 10 = 6 marks

TOTAL FOR SECTION C = 16 MARKS

Section D: The cardiovascular system for sports performance

Answer ALL questions. Write your answers in the spaces provided.

Guided

11 | During a circuit training session, performers work maximally and then have a recovery period before moving on to the next station.

(a) Oxygen delivery and removal of waste products are essential to maintain performance in circuit training. Explain **one other** role of the cardiovascular system during an exercise session.

4 marks

> Note how the question asks for **one other** role. Do not use the roles given in the question in your answer.

Another role of the cardiovascular system during exercise

is thermoregulation ....

....

....

....

....

....

> Heart rate can be recorded during circuit training to monitor the impact of the exercise on heart rate.

(b) (i) Complete the graph to show the likely changes in heart rate during a typical circuit session.

2 marks

> Remember, **you can only work with the data you have**. You are not told the age of the performer, so you cannot work out their maximum heart rate. However, you are given some information at the beginning of the question – you are told they work maximally at the station and then have time for recovery between stations. What will happen to their heart rate when working flat out? What will happen when they stop?

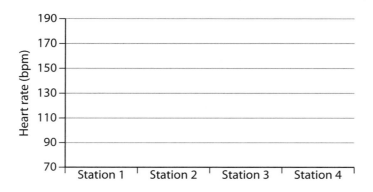

Guided

(b) (ii) Describe the likely changes in heart rate after the final station in the circuit, during the first five minutes of recovery.

2 marks

Immediately after the exercise there should be a steep drop in heart rate at first, although this

will gradually ....

....

....

Guided

(c)   Explain the nervous control of the heart that allows us to regulate our heart rate during exercise.

5 marks

🔗 **Links**   For more on nervous control of the cardiac cycle look at page 31 of the Revision Guide.

The sinoatrial node acts as a ...., controlling how quickly the

heart contracts. ....

....

Therefore, by controlling the rate that these electrical impulses are sent ....

....

....

....

The parasympathetic nervous system sends messages to the sinoatrial node to ....

heart rate during less intense exercise. ....

....

Total for Question 11 = 13 marks

12 Explain why it is necessary for veins to have valves in order to achieve their function.

3 marks

Remember, veins return blood to the heart. Think about their characteristics. Why are they the only type of blood vessel that needs valves?

....

....

....

....

....

....

Total for Question 12 = 3 marks

> **Guided** > **13** | Benji wanted to increase his fitness so joined a fitness class. Before taking the class for the first time, the instructor asked Benji to complete a questionnaire about his health.

Assess the importance to cardiovascular health of completing a medical check before undertaking strenuous exercise for the first time.

6 marks

Plan:

Purpose of medical check – why it is important? Examples

Relevance of strenuous activity

How might cardiovascular health be affected if no medical check, include examples

Judgement

A medical check is carried out by the organisers of the fitness class to check to see if Benji has any

....

....

For example, if Benji has high blood pressure, as he exercises his blood pressure will increase

further in response to the exercise, ...

....

....

....

....

Although for most people medical screening does not show any health conditions that the

organisers and individual need to be aware of, for those with an existing cardiovascular health

condition medical screening is essential as ....

....

....

Total for Question 13 = 6 marks

TOTAL FOR SECTION D = 22 MARKS

Section E: Energy systems for sports performance

Answer ALL questions. Write your answers in the spaces provided.

14 Participation in sport requires a constant supply of energy.

(a) Describe the process of ATP resynthesis via the lactate system.

4 marks

Remember the lactate system is **anaerobic**.

Links For information on the lactate system look at page 37 of the Revision Guide.

....
....
....
....
....
....
....
....

Guided

(b) Explain why the lactate system would be of limited use in activities lasting over 2–3 minutes.

3 marks

Why would the lactate system be of limited use? Complete the paragraph provided to give a clear explanation.

The lactate system can only be used for a limited

amount of time because the waste products of anaerobic glycolysis, such as ....,

increase the .... of the blood, making it more difficult to continue with

energy production, causing muscle ....

Total for Question 14 = 7 marks

15 Explain how diabetes could impact on performance in endurance activities, such as triathlons or iron man competitions.

3 marks

Note the question context: 'endurance activities'. Remember those with diabetes are unable to regulate blood glucose levels. How might this impact on performance in endurance events?

....
....
....
....
....

Total for Question 15 = 3 marks

16 | The 10 000 m race is run over 25 laps of the track.

Assess the impact of adaptations of the energy systems on performance in a 10 000 m race. **6 marks**

Look at the **question context**. A specific energy system has not been mentioned, so you need to consider **all three** in your answer. However, you are told this is in the context of a long-distance race, so make sure you apply your answer to this context. The command word is **assess**, so make a judgement about the importance of these adaptations.

Links See page 43 of the Revision Guide for further guidance on how to approach long-answer questions.

....

....

....

....

....

....

....

....

....

....

....

Therefore, although adaptations to each energy system can be advantageous to the long-distance runner, the most significant adaptations in terms of performance are on the aerobic energy system due to the time taken to complete the race.

Total for Question 16 = 6 marks

TOTAL FOR SECTION E = 16 MARKS

Section F: Interrelationships between body systems for sports performance

Answer the question. Write your answer in the space provided.

Guided

17 To what extent do the muscular and cardiovascular systems need to work together to allow good performance in activities such as a 90-minute game of football?

8 marks

This question requires you to demonstrate your knowledge of how **two or more** body systems work together during sport and exercise. Examples of possible combinations might be muscular and energy systems, cardiovascular and respiratory systems, energy and cardiovascular systems.

Plan:

Role of muscular system in sport and exercise

Role of cardiovascular system in sport and exercise

Overlap between systems — how one allows the other to 'do its job'

Consequences if they don't work together

....

....

....

....

....

....

....

....

....

....

....

....

....

....

....

....

Total for Question 17 = 8 marks

TOTAL FOR SECTION F = 8 MARKS

END OF PAPER 1   **TOTAL FOR PAPER = 90 MARKS**

Revision test 2

This Workbook is designed to revise the skills that might be needed in your exam. The details of the actual exam may change, so make sure you are up to date. Ask your tutor or check the Pearson website for the most up-to-date Sample Assessment Material to get an idea of the structure of the exam and what this requires of you.

Section A: Skeletal system for sports performance

Answer ALL questions. Write your answers in the spaces provided.

1   Synovial joints are important to sports performers because they allow movement to complete sport and exercise.

The picture shows a synovial joint.

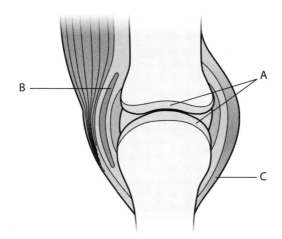

(a)   Identify the components A and B.

`2 marks`

....

....

(b)   Explain, using an example, the importance of the component labelled C to a sports performer.

`4 marks`

....

....

....

....

> Although the question doesn't specifically ask you to name 'C' from the picture it is a good idea to do so, to make it clear that you know the name of the structure you are explaining the importance of.

....

....

....

....

....

Total for Question 1 = 6 marks

2 The picture shows a high jumper attempting to clear the bar.

Analyse how the cartilaginous joints of the upper and lower skeleton allow the high jumper to clear the bar.

`6 marks`

For an essay-style question, it is a good idea to produce a quick plan before starting to write your response. Use this plan to attempt the question:

• What are the cartilaginous joints in the upper and lower skeleton?

• Structure – irregular shape, with cartilage between each vertebrae

• Shape/structure linked to range of movement – limited movement individually but greater range when the whole spine is considered

• Links to performance of technique – what movement is required in high jump/in picture, problems for performer if unable to use this range of movement.

....

....

....

....

....

....

....

....

....

....

....

....

Total for Question 2 = 6 marks

TOTAL FOR SECTION A = 12 MARKS

Section B: Muscular system for sports performance

Answer ALL questions. Write your answers in the spaces provided.

3 Sometimes during or after an exercise session, an athlete can experience cramp.

(a) Describe what happens to the athlete when they experience cramp.

2 marks

....

....

....

....

(b) Apart from taking on sufficient water, how else can an athlete reduce the risk of getting cramp?

1 mark

....

....

Total for Question 3 = 3 marks

4 | The picture shows a swimmer as he starts a race.

(a) Analyse the antagonistic muscle action at the ankle **and** the knee of the shaded leg, which results in the swimmer pushing off the blocks to start the race.

`4 marks`

> Make sure you read the question carefully. Your answer to this question must focus on the **antagonistic pair of muscles** working at the ankle and knee of the **shaded leg only**. There is no need to reference the other leg.

> **Links** See pages 8 and 15 of the Revision Guide for more on flexion, dorsiflexion and antagonistic muscle pairs.

....

....

....

....

....

....

....

....

(b) Explain which muscle fibre type would be used to propel the swimmer from the blocks.

`3 marks`

....

....

....

....

....

....

Total for Question 4 = 7 marks

5 Jacob trains regularly to improve his fitness for basketball.
The picture shows Jacob attempting to score a basket.

Discuss the importance of adaptations to Jacob's muscular system in improving his basketball performance.

6 marks

This question asks for a **discussion**. You will need to consider the adaptations to the muscular system and whether these will have any potential impact on Jacob's performance. Use the picture to help.

Links See page 43 of the Revision Guide for further guidance on how to approach long-answer questions.

....

....

....

....

....

....

....

....

....

....

....

....

Total for Question 5 = 6 marks

TOTAL FOR SECTION B = 16 MARKS

Section C: The respiratory system for sports performance

Answer ALL questions. Write your answers in the spaces provided.

6 It is important during a sport and exercise session to have the required oxygen for the activity.

(a) Describe the pathway of air as it leaves the trachea en route to the capillaries in the lungs.

`4 marks`

....

....

....

....

....

....

....

(b) Explain how the diaphragm and the intercostal muscles ensure sufficient air can be breathed in to the lungs during exercise.

`3 marks`

> Note the question is only asking about **breathing in**. Therefore, you do not need to make any reference to the muscle action during expiration.

....

....

....

....

....

....

Total for Question 6 = 7 marks

7 (a) Define the term 'vital capacity'.

`1 mark`

....

....

(b) Name the other lung volume that combines with vital capacity to give a performer's total lung capacity.

`1 mark`

....

(c) State **one** advantage of an increased vital capacity for a performer.

`1 mark`

....

Total for Question 7 = 3 marks

8 A standard Olympic triathlon is a continuous race involving a 1500 m swim, a 40 km cycle ride and a 10 km run. Elite female triathletes will take approximately two hours to complete the race.

The respiratory system responds to exercise. Assess the impact of these responses on the level of gaseous exchange and the relevance of this to a triathlete during their event.

6 marks

Try to break down the question when planning your answer. You could do this by asking yourself several smaller questions, such as: what is gaseous exchange? What are the immediate responses of the respiratory system to exercise? Why is gaseous exchange important in a triathlon? How will the responses impact on gaseous exchange and what impact will this have on performance in a triathlon?

....

....

....

....

....

....

....

....

....

....

....

....

Total for Question 8 = 6 marks

TOTAL FOR SECTION C = 16 MARKS

Section D: The cardiovascular system for sports performance

Answer ALL questions. Write your answers in the spaces provided.

9   The heart is responsible for the delivery of oxygen and the nutrients required for sport and exercise. The picture shows a view of the heart.

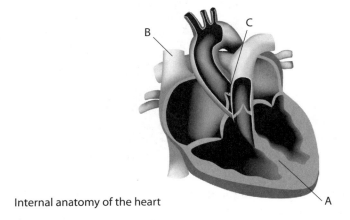

Internal anatomy of the heart

🔗 **Links**   See page 28 of the Revision Guide for more on the heart.

(a)   Identify the components A and B.

2 marks

....

....

(b)   Explain the importance of the component labelled C to a sports performer.

4 marks

> Although the question doesn't specifically ask you to name 'C' from the picture, it is always a good idea to do so, to make it clear that you know the name of the structure you are explaining the importance of.

....

....

....

....

....

....

(c)   Explain how the heart ensures an elevated level of oxygen is available for the performer even before exercise begins.

3 marks

....

....

....

....

Total for Question 9 = 9 marks

10 During exercise it is essential to control the flow of blood.
The pie chart shows the proportion of blood flow to the skin at rest compared to during exercise.

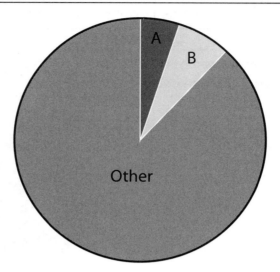

(a) Explain which segment of the pie chart, A or B, represents blood flow to the skin during exercise.

3 marks

Don't worry about the category 'other' as this has not been referenced in the question. This simply refers to the proportion of blood flow to other areas of the body.

....

....

....

....

....

....

(b) Describe how blood flow is redistributed to the skin.

3 marks

....

....

....

....

....

....

(c) State the impact on performance if an athlete was unable to regulate blood flow in this way.

1 mark

....

....

Total for Question 10 = 7 marks

11 | Blood vessels have different characteristics depending on their function, but all blood vessels contribute to the delivery of oxygen and removal of waste products required during exercise.

The graph shows:

• the velocity of the blood as it passes through each vessel

• the blood pressure as the blood passes through each vessel.

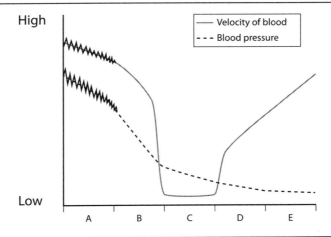

Links See page 29 of the Revision Guide for information on blood vessels.

Analyse the graph to determine the different blood vessel types represented by the letters A, B, C, D and E, justifying your answer in relation to their function in exercise.

6 marks

Think about the information you are given in the graph and how you can use it in your answer. Why is it useful to know the speed of the blood flow? Which type of vessels have blood travelling at the fastest speed? How is blood pressure useful? Do different blood vessels have different blood pressures? What is the significance of the zigzag lines in the first column?

....

....

....

....

....

....

....

....

....

....

....

....

Total for Question 11 = 6 marks

TOTAL FOR SECTION D = 22 MARKS

Section E: Energy systems for sports performance

Answer ALL questions. Write your answers in the spaces provided.

---

12 Participation in sport requires a constant supply of energy.

(a) Identify the chemical source of fuel in the ATP-PC system.

`1 mark`

....

....

(b) State how this chemical source of fuel is used in the ATP-PC system.

`1 mark`

....

....

Total for Question 12 = 2 marks

---

13 Explain why lactate is produced in the lactate energy system.

`3 marks`

....

....

....

....

....

....

Total for Question 13 = 3 marks

---

14 Identify the energy system that provides the greatest yield of ATP.

`1 mark`

....

....

> Remember 'yield' in this context means the amount, so which energy system will give the most ATP?

Total for Question 14 = 1 mark

15 Tour de France cyclists will use, on average, 6000 calories a day which is three times as much as a normal person. This goes up to 8000 calories during the mountain stages of the race.

Explain why it is necessary that each stage of the race has a feed station, where riders can take food and drinks from their support team standing by the side of the road.

4 marks

....

....

....

....

....

....

....

....

Total for Question 15 = 4 marks

16 The 400 m is considered a sprint event. Elite male athletes complete this race in under 50 seconds.

Evaluate the contribution of each energy system to a 400 m runner.

6 marks

Look at the question context – a specific energy system has not been mentioned, so you should consider all three in your answer. Is one system more important than another to the 400 m runner? If so, why?

Links See pages 36, 37 and 38 of the Revision Guide for information on the different energy systems.

....
....
....
....
....
....
....
....
....
....
....
....

Total for Question 16 = 6 marks

TOTAL FOR SECTION E = 16 MARKS

Section F: Interrelationships between body systems for sports performance

Answer the question. Write your answer in the space provided.

17 To what extent do the adaptations to the respiratory and aerobic energy systems contribute to improved performance in endurance events?

8 marks

This question requires you to demonstrate your knowledge of **how two or more body systems work together** during sport and exercise. Examples might be the muscular and cardiovascular system, energy and respiratory systems, or any other combination.

....

....

....

....

....

....

....

....

....

....

....

....

....

....

....

Total for Question 17 = 8 marks

TOTAL FOR SECTION F = 8 MARKS

END OF PAPER 2
TOTAL FOR PAPER = 90 MARKS

Unit 2: Fitness Training and Programming for Health, Sport and Well-being

Your task

Unit 2 will be assessed through a task, which will be set by Pearson. You will need to use your ability to interpret lifestyle factors and health screening data from a scenario and additional information, in order to develop and justify a fitness training programme and nutritional advice based on these interpretations. You will answer questions based on the given scenario and the notes and information you have gathered.

Your Revision Workbook

This Workbook is designed to **revise skills** that might be needed in your assessed task. The details of your actual assessed task may change from year to year so always make sure you are up to date. Ask your tutor or check the **Pearson website** for the most up-to-date **Sample Assessment Material** to get an idea of the structure of your assessed task and what this requires of you.

To support your revision, this Workbook contains revision tasks to help you revise the skills that might be needed in your assessed task. These revision tasks are divided into sections.

Gathering information and making notes

In your Workbook you will use your skills to:
- Read the task information and make notes on key information about the client in the scenario (pages 32 and 52)
- Gather information to prepare background notes on lifestyle factors and screening processes; lifestyle modification techniques; nutritional guidance and training methods (pages 33–38 and 53–56)
- Prepare background notes on designing a training programme for the client (pages 39–41 and 57–59)

Reviewing additional information

You will then use your skills to:
- Review the additional information (pages 42–45 and 60–63)
- Use this and your preparatory notes to go on and answer the questions

Responding to questions

Your response to the questions will help you to revise:
- **Interpreting** lifestyle factors and screening information for the client (pages 46 and 64)
- **Developing** and **justifying** lifestyle and nutritional guidance for the client in the task information scenario, using screening information, your research and your own knowledge (pages 47–48 and 65–66)
- **Developing** a fitness programme for the client (pages 49–50 and 67–69)
- **Justifying** your fitness programme (pages 51 and 70)

Links To help you revise skills that might be needed in your Unit 2 task, this Workbook contains two sets of revision tasks starting on pages 31 and 52. The first is guided and models good techniques, to help you develop your skills. The second offers less guidance as you apply your skills. See the introduction on page iii for more information on features included to help you revise.

Revision task 1

To support your revision, this Workbook contains revision tasks to help you revise the skills that might be needed in your assessed task. The details of the actual assessed task may change so always make sure you are up to date. Ask your tutor or check the Pearson website for the most up-to-date Sample Assessment Material to get an idea of the structure of your exam and what this requires of you.

Planning your time

When gathering information and making notes, you need to plan your time carefully. Estimate how long you will need for each part, so that you can complete your notes within the allocated time. Fill in the table below to help you plan your background preparation.

Task	Time allocation
Read the task information carefully and **highlight key information**	
Prepare notes on **lifestyle factors and screening processes**	
Prepare notes on **lifestyle modification techniques**	
Prepare notes on **nutritional guidance**	
Prepare notes on **training methods**	
Prepare notes on **designing a training programme**	
Prepare notes on **justifying your training programme**	

When making your notes you might want to consider areas such as:

- recommendations to promote health and well-being
- lifestyle factors and their effect on health and well-being
- nutritional programming requirements
- screening processes for training programming, including health monitoring tests
- training methods for different components of fitness
- principles of fitness training
- appropriate training activities to meet the needs of the individual.

The following pages are divided into sections covering each of these note-taking themes.

Using preparatory notes
In this Revision Workbook you can refer to any of the notes you have made as you give answers to the questions. Check with your tutor or look at the most up-to-date Sample Assessment Materials to see whether you can refer to your notes **in your actual assessment** or whether there are any restrictions on them.

Reading the task information

> Make sure you **read the task information thoroughly**. Perhaps read the scenario as a whole, then read it again and highlight what you think is the key information about the client. Being clear on the task information from the outset will ensure that you fully understand your client and conduct the appropriate research and preparation for answering the questions.

Task information

Scenario

Mr Sharp is 30 years old. He works as a science teacher at a high school. He works from 8.30 am until 3.30 pm, but often has to do more work when he gets home. He has 45 minutes for lunch, but this is often a working lunch where he attends various meetings. He occasionally car shares the travel to and from work, a distance of 5 miles.

He has recently noticed that he is gaining weight, which is making him start to feel down. His colleagues at work have asked him to join their 5-a-side football team which starts playing their league fixtures in 6 weeks' time. He currently takes part in no exercise.

Mr Sharp decides to join the school gym and takes part in a fitness assessment. He is then given a 6 week training programme to follow.

Mr Sharp has previously completed a PAR-Q and has indicated that he has no medical conditions and is fit to take part in activity.

Fill out the notes below to understand Mr Sharp's key information.

Guided

1   Consider Mr Sharp's age.

   30 years old, no medical conditions so able to participate in a range of types of exercise, although currently not exercising at all.

2   Write down key points of Mr Sharp's occupation.

   ....

   ....

3   Consider whether exercise can be incorporated in the journey to and from work.

   When it is not Mr Sharp's day to drive, he could get a lift to work and then run, cycle, walk home; on the journey home he would be less restricted for time.

4   Are Mr Sharp's lunch breaks an opportunity for incorporating exercise?

   ....

5   Consider Mr Sharp's current physical fitness.

   ....

6   Consider Mr Sharp's goal.

   To join the school 5-a-side football team, fixtures start in 6 weeks.

> 🔗 **Links**   For more help with reading the task information revisit page 85 of the Revision Guide.

Gathering information

Making notes on lifestyle factors and screening processes

This page shows exemplar notes on **lifestyle factors** and **screening processes**. Some areas have been left blank for you to complete. You will make use of these notes when responding to Question 1, on page 46.

Think about all the lifestyle factors that may be relevant to your scenario. You should **bullet-point** your notes and you might find it useful to organise them under headings like the ones below. Complete the notes below to help you do this.

Mr Sharp: **positive lifestyle factors** – wants to start exercising.

Physical activity

• No exercise therefore not meeting government recommendations.

• Physical health benefits:

  ....

  ....

  ....

• Psychological health benefits:

  ....

  ....

  ....

Smoking

If Mr Sharp smokes, think about:

• Health risks: lung-related conditions (COPD, bronchitis); heart-related conditions (heart disease/ attack, stroke); other health-related conditions (prolonged symptoms of asthma, infertility).

• 5 health benefits of stopping: ....

  ....

  ....

Alcohol

Does Mr Sharp drink alcohol? If so:

• Government recommends ___ units.

• Short-term effects: nausea, vomiting, blackouts.

• Long-term effects: ....;..............................;..............................;

• Mental health problems: stress, depression, poor sleep pattern.

• Empty calories – alcohol has no nutritional value, affects weight.

Stress

• Could Mr Sharp suffer from stress?

• Possible stress from teaching.

• Long-term effects: ....;..............................;

  ....;..............................;

Sleep

- Recommendation is _____ hours per night.
- Required for muscle repair, memory consolidation and release of hormones regulating growth and appetite.
- Effects of poor sleep: ....; ....; ....; ....; ....

Diet

- Eat Well Plate recommendations: plenty of fruit/veg, plenty of e.g. potatoes/bread/rice, some dairy products, some meat/fish, a small amount of foods/drinks high in fat/sugar (consider whether balanced/unbalanced), eating the right amount/eating a variety of foods.
- Consider timing of meals, number of meals, food choices, alcohol intake, portion sizes, food organisation/preparation, eating slower.
- Benefits of a healthy diet: ....; ....; ....; ....; ....

BMI

- Less than 18.5 = underweight.
- 18.5–24.9 = ...
- 25–29.9 =overweight.
- 30–39.9 = obese.
- 40 or more = very obese.
- Can cause health issues: high BP, diabetes.

Waist-to-hip ratio

- 0.95 and below = low risk.
- 0.96–1.0 = ...
- 1.0+ = high risk.
- Excessive weight around the waist increases risk of some diseases.

Resting heart rate

- Factors that affect heart rate: caffeine and alcohol, exercise, disease and drugs.

	RESTING HEART RATE AGED 26–35
ATHLETE	....
EXCELLENT	....
GOOD	....
ABOVE AVERAGE	66–70
AVERAGE	71–74
BELOW AVERAGE	75–81
POOR	82+

Blood pressure

- Blood pressure graph could be drawn here.
- Risks associated with high BP: ....; ....; ....; ....

Making notes on lifestyle modification techniques

 This page shows exemplar notes on **lifestyle modification techniques**. Some areas have been left blank for you to complete. You will make use of these notes when responding to Question 2, on page 47.

Think about all the lifestyle modification techniques that may be relevant to your scenario.

Physical activity

- Recommendations for Mr Sharp: 30 min, 5 times per week.

- Moderate/vigorous exercise for 75 min spread across the week.

- Strength training: .... per week

- Strategies to overcome time barrier: prioritise, manage daily routine, indentify available time slots, incorporate into daily routine, start a new activity, select an activity that doesn't take much time.

- Strategies to overcome the cost barrier: ....; ....

- Strategies to overcome the transport/location barrier: park further away and walk, use local walks.

- Strategies to overcome the lack of energy/motivation: ....;

   ....; ....; ....;

   ....; ....

- Strategies to overcome the family barrier: exercise with the kids, exercise at home.

Smoking

If Mr Sharp smokes recommend the following:

- Self-help tips: plan to quit – identify when he craves cigarettes and break the habit, improved diet, drinking less and exercise changes will all work in combination to reduce smoking.

- NHS smoking helpline – free support.

- NRT: patches, chewing gum, etc.

- Negatives of NRT: expensive, possible side effects – skin irritation, disturbed sleep, upset stomach.

Alcohol

If Mr Sharp consumes above the recommended 14 units per week:

- Self-help tips: break habit – encourage him to do something different when he would usually drink, have drink-free days, pace/space drinks, have smaller drinks.

- Tips for reducing drinking at home: ....; ....; ....

- Reduce drinking while out: set a limit, opt out of rounds, budget for a fixed amount.

- External help: self-help groups, AA, drinkline, counselling, meditation, yoga.

Stress

An improved lifestyle may reduce stress levels.

Sleep

- Recommended amount: .... hours.

- An improved lifestyle may encourage extra sleep.

<u>Diet</u>

- Use the Eat Well Plate to achieve a balanced diet, incorporating the right proportion and a wide variety of foods.
- Consider the .... of meals.
- Number of meals.
- Food choices – consider whether he needs healthier choices for all meals/snacks.
- Consider .... intake.
- Consider alcohol intake.
- Consider caffeine intake.
- Consider portion sizes.
- Better preparation and organisation of meals/snacks.

<u>Resting heart rate</u>

If RHR is average or below average, recommend:

- less alcohol and caffeine
- more exercise.

<u>BMI/waist-to-hip ratio</u>

If BMI/WHR is high, recommend:

- healthier eating/balanced diet
- increasing ....
- drinking more fluids.

<u>Blood pressure</u>

If BP is high, recommend the following for treatment/prevention: less salt, more fruit and veg, maintaining a healthy weight, drinking less alcohol, more exercise, stopping smoking, reducing intake of coffee, tea.

Making notes on nutritional guidance

 This page shows exemplar notes on **nutritional guidance**. Some areas have been left blank for you to complete. You will make use of these notes when responding to Question 3, on page 48.

Think about all the nutritional guidance that could be relevant to your scenario.

Mr Sharp: currently possible **positive energy balance** – i.e. putting more energy (food) into his body than using (no exercise).

Eat Well Plate

• Ensure reference to the Eat Well Plate.

• Plenty of fruit/veg: incorporate through all meals/snacks.

• Plenty of potatoes, bread, rice, etc: perhaps encourage brown or whole grain options and cereal.

• Some .... and .... : through cereal for breakfast, yoghurts, etc.

• Some meat, fish etc – choose white meats when possible.

• Small amounts of food/drink high in fat/sugar.

Strategies for Mr Sharp

• Consider timing of meals: does Mr Sharp eat too late/early; could he eat sooner/later? Prepare meals the night before, freeze meals to use quickly with a busy career.

• Number of meals: does Mr Sharp miss any meals? If he does, he needs to be encouraged ....

....

• Food choices – refer to his food diary. Does he need to consider healthier choices – e.g. avoid mayonnaise or choose low-fat option, incorporate salad, swap crisps for nuts, add fruit to yoghurt.

• Avoid takeaways, as high in fat – prepare own version at home.

• Healthier snacks: avoid crisps, chocolate, biscuits and incorporate more fruit, cereal bars and nuts.

• Be better prepared and organised – snacks and meals could be ....

....

....

• Look at food labels to check for healthier alternatives.

• Consider portion sizes.

Fluid intake

• Consider fluid intake for Mr Sharp. Does he achieve the 2–2.5 litres per day? May need to .... when exercising.

• Water is an adequate choice of fluid.

• Caffeine needs to be in moderation. Maximum recommendation is ....
It could be beneficial to reduce caffeine intake.

Making notes on training methods

 Guided ⟩ This page shows exemplar notes on **training methods**. Some areas have been left blank for you to complete. You will make use of these notes when responding to Question 4, on page 49.

Think about all the training methods that could be relevant to your scenario.

<u>Overview</u>

- 1st goal to start exercise and progress to achieving the government recommendation of at least 150 min of moderate activity per week.
- Or 75 min of vigorous exercise spread across the week.
- Strength training – twice a week.
- 2nd goal to participate in 5-a-side football league.
- Mr Sharp = beginner.

<u>Frequency</u>

Begin with .... and increase to ....

<u>Intensity</u>

- Low intensity to begin with: ....% heart-rate training zone.
- Progress to 60–70% over 6 weeks.

<u>Time</u>

Begin with 20–30 min and progress over 6 weeks.

<u>Type</u>

- Provide a 'cross train' programme for Mr Sharp – a range of training methods – balanced conditioning, avoid boredom and injuries.
- Goal is to partake in ...., so activities need to mimic the sport with more ....

....

<u>Fartlek training</u>

- Intensity varies: walk, jog, sprint (like football).
- Changes in direction (like football).
- Changes in pace (like football).
- No rest periods.
- Can be outdoor/indoor.

<u>Advantages:</u>

- Easy to use – Mr Sharp (beginner).
- Easy to adapt to the sport.
- Boredom reduced with this method.
- Good for sports with a change of pace.

<u>Interval training</u>

- Work/rest/work periods.
- Changes in pace (like football).
- Can be outdoor/indoor.

<u>Advantages:</u>

....

....

<u>Circuit training</u>

- Can combine aerobic, muscular and strength training.
- Could be used to incorporate some strength training into Mr Sharp's lifestyle.
- Structured to individual's training needs.
- Rest periods.

<u>Advantages:</u>

....

....

....

Making notes on designing a training programme

Guided

 This page shows exemplar notes on **designing a training programme**. Some areas have been left blank for you to complete. You will make use of these notes when responding to Question 5, on page 50, when designing training for the selected individual.

Week 1: rest days – Thursday and Saturday; training – Monday and Wednesday; light activities – Tuesday, Friday, Sunday (20-min fast walk at lunch).

	Mon	Wed
Physical activity	Gym session Warm-up: .... Main activity: 15 min (fartlek): • 2-min run with 1-min fast walk – aim for HR of 95 bpm (50% of MHR). • Repeat 5 times. Strengthening section: • knee extension (quads) – 12 reps, 2 sets, weight 20 kg (45-sec rest) • leg curl hamstring – 12 reps, 2 sets, weight 15 kg (45-sec rest) • calf raises – 12 reps, 2 sets with 5 kg dumbbells (45-sec rest) • crunches – 12 reps, 2 sets (30-sec rest) • reverse crunches – 12 reps, 2 sets, 30-sec rest. Cool-down:	Outdoor session – school Astro Turf Warm-up: jog for 5 min. Main activity: 20 min 40 sec (fartlek): • jog for 1 min • run hard ($\frac{3}{4}$ pace) for 30 sec • jog for 1 min • sprint for 10 sec • jog for 1 min • run backwards for 30 sec • jog for 1 min • repeat 4 times • aim for HR of 95 bpm (50% of MHR). Flexibility section: .... Cool-down: 5-min walk.

Week 3: rest days – Thursday and Saturday; training – Monday, Wednesday, Friday; light activities – Tuesday, Sunday.

Gym session

• Increase HR rather than duration of fartlek (60% – 114 bpm).

• Increase reps to 15.

Outdoor session

• Increase HR rather than duration of fartlek (60% – 114 bpm).

• Increase stretches to 8 sec, then repeat for 10 sec.

Add another session – Friday: circuit training:

• Warm-up – 5-min jog around sports hall, 8 stations.

• Main circuit part 1 – 1 min on each (45-sec rest); circuit part 2 – 45 sec on each (30-sec rest); circuit part 3 – 30 sec on each (15-sec rest). (Wall volley (ball), squats, press ups, lunges, shuttle runs – 10 m dribbling with a football, crunches with a football, burpees, hurdles.)

• Cool-down – 5 mins, jog reducing pace to a walk.

Week 6: rest days – Thursday and Saturday; training – Monday, Wednesday, Friday, Sunday; light activities – Tuesday.

<u>Gym session</u>

- Increase HR rather than duration of fartlek (70% – 133 bpm).
- Increase sets to 3, reduce reps to 12.

<u>Outdoor session</u>

- Increase HR rather than duration of fartlek (70% – 133 bpm).
- Increase stretches to 10 sec, then repeat for 12 sec.

<u>Circuit session</u>

- Decrease rest period by 10 sec (e.g. part 1 = 35-sec rest; part 2 = 20-sec rest; part 3 = 5-sec rest).

<u>Add another session</u> – Sunday: possibly football-related skills/speed/agility/interval training.

Making notes on justifying your training programme

This page shows exemplar notes on **justifying your training programme**. Some areas have been left blank for you to complete. You will make use of these notes when responding to Question 6, on page 51.

- All sessions have a warm-up, main activity and cool-down.

Frequency

- Week 1: two training sessions; week 3: three training sessions; week 6: four training sessions.
- **Progressed** frequency – gradually to avoid overtraining, injury.

Intensity

- Beginner, so low intensity to begin with, progressing to intensity of weeks 3 and 6.
- Heart-rate training suitable for Mr Sharp (new to training – **individual needs**).
- Strength training – reps/weight/sets/recovery suitable for Mr Sharp's **individual needs**.
- Flexibility – stretches duration suitable for Mr Sharp's **individual needs**.
- Week 3 – increased heart rate so Mr Sharp is working harder – **progression/overload**.
    - Reps only changed in strength training – important not to change too much too soon – **progression/overload**.
    - Duration of stretches in flexibility session increased – same stretches used to ensure development – **progression/overload**.
- Week 6 – again heart rate increase – **progression/overload**.
    - Increase sets to 3 and reduce reps – **progression/overload**.
    - Increase duration of stretches – **progression/overload**.
    - Extra session progresses to mimic specific movements in football.

Time

- Sessions lasting approx 40 min
- 20 min of aerobic training is an optimal timeframe.

Type

- Training sessions – **variation** of aerobic, strength, flexibility, agility sessions. Suitable for football.
- Circuit training incorporates football to offer variety, **specificity** and fun.
- Flexibility and strength – **specifically** concentrating on ....

    .... – ....

- Light activities – to work towards incorporating more activity into Mr Sharp's lifestyle to achieve government recommendations.

Principles of training

Rest and recuperation – always .... days to allow for growth and repair.

- Overload – ensure that Mr Sharp is working above what he is used to, especially in week 1 as he was completing no exercise prior to this; continue to overload by changing FITT principles.
- **Progression** – in activities over the 6 weeks: factors are manipulated to ensure progression e.g.

    ...., ... and ....

- **Individual needs** – planned specifically to Mr Sharp's aim/level of fitness and sport, and possible access to school facilities.
- **Variation** – the sessions are varied and include .... , to avoid boredom.
- **Adaptation** – actions will become easier and body will adapt.

Reviewing additional information

If you are provided with additional information, read the information carefully and use this and your notes to interpret the needs of the individual in order to prepare guidance on lifestyle, nutrition and fitness training.

Personal details

Section 1: Personal details

Name: **Mr M Sharp**
Address: **25 Shear Brow**
           Anytown
Home telephone: **01234 567890**
Mobile telephone: **07123456789**
Email: **msharp@email.com**
Date of birth: **01/01/1986**
Please answer the following questions to the best of your knowledge.
Occupation

1. What is your occupation?
    Science teacher
2. How many hours do you work weekly?
    8.30 am–3.30 pm with 45 min for lunch, plus planning and marking
3. How far do you live from your workplace?
    5 miles
4. How do you travel to work?
    Car (share on a Tuesday and Thursday only)

Current activity levels

Section 2: Current activity levels

1. How many times a week do you currently take part in physical activity?
    None

Make sure you read the lifestyle questionnaire thoroughly and highlight key and new information. Being clear about your client from the outset will ensure that you answer the questions appropriately. Fill in the notes below to help you.

1 Justify the number of sessions of physical activity per week you would recommend for Mr Sharp.

....

....

Links For more help with interpreting the lifestyle questionnaire revisit page 53 of the Revision Guide.

Nutritional status

> When interpreting someone's nutritional intake, remember to consider the following aspects:
> the Eat Well Plate/food choices, fluid intake, timing and number of meals, portion sizes, organisation and preparation, training needs.

Section 3: Nutritional status

1. How many meals do you have each day? **3**
2. Do you take any supplements? If yes, which ones? **No**

Day 1	Breakfast	Lunch	Dinner	Snacks
Y/N	N	Y	Y	Y
Time of day		12.30 pm	7 pm	Mid-morning Mid-afternoon Evening
Food intake		Chicken mayo baguette Crisps Yoghurt	Sausage, mash and carrots	Cereal bar Biscuit Crisps
Fluid intake	Tea x 2 cups, coffee x 1 cup, can of coke, 2 pints of beer			
Day 2	Breakfast	Lunch	Dinner	Snacks
Y/N	N	Y	Y	Y
Time of day		12.30 pm	7 pm	Mid-morning Mid-afternoon Evening
Food intake		Ham and cheese panini Apple Yoghurt	Takeaway – chicken kebab and chips	Cereal bar Biscuit Popcorn
Fluid intake	Tea x 2 cups, coffee x 1 cup, can of coke, 2 pints of beer			

> **Guided**
>
> When analysing an individual's nutritional status, look at the key issues with their eating and drinking habits. Complete the notes below to help you think about this.
>
> 1 Looking at **day 1**, what are the key issues with Mr Sharp's eating and drinking habits?
>
> • No breakfast, no fruit and limited vegetables, crisps/biscuits.
>
> • Not achieving recommended hydration levels, alcohol intake (if continued) for rest of week could be above recommendations.
>
> 2 Looking at **day 2**, what are the key issues with Mr Sharp's eating and drinking habits?
>
> ....
>
> ....

> **Links** For more help with providing nutritional guidance revisit pages 58–64 and 89 of the Revision Guide.

Your lifestyle

Section 4: Your lifestyle

> **Please answer the following questions to the best of your knowledge.**
> 1. How many units of alcohol do you drink in a typical week? **20**
> 2. Do you smoke? **Yes** If yes, how many a day? **10**
> 3. Do you experience stress on a daily basis? **Yes**
> 4. If yes, what causes you stress (if you know)? **School deadlines**
> 5. On average, how many hours sleep do you get per night? **7**

Health monitoring tests – test results

Section 5: Health monitoring tests – test results

Test	Result
Blood pressure	135/85 mmHg
Resting heart rate	74 bpm
Body mass index	28
Waist-to-hip ratio	1.0

Physical activity/sporting goals

Section 6: Physical activity/sporting goals

> 1. What are your physical activity/sporting goals?
>   **Take part in 5-a-side football league in 6 weeks.**

CLIENT DECLARATION

I have understood and answered all of the above questions honestly.

Signed Client: **MSharp**   Print Name: **Matthew Sharp**   Date: **01/04/16**

When interpreting your individual's lifestyle factors, you will need to use your preparatory notes. From this you will be able to establish the individual's strengths and areas for improvement, and compare their responses/results to government recommendations, guidelines and normative data. Answer the questions below to help you.

 1 Mr Sharp has indicated that he consumes **20** units of alcohol per week. Interpret this response.

....

....

2 Mr Sharp's blood pressure has been measured at **135/85 mmHg**. Interpret this result.

....

....

Links For more help with interpreting lifestyle factors revisit pages 44–52 of the Revision Guide. For interpreting the results of health monitoring tests revisit pages 54–57 of the Revision Guide.

Using preparatory notes

In this Revision Workbook you can refer to any of the notes you have made as you give answers to the questions (pages 46–51). Check with your tutor or look at the most up-to-date Sample Assessment Materials to see whether you can refer to your notes **in your actual assessment** or whether there are any restrictions on them.

Questions

> All questions relate to the task information featuring Mr Sharp. In your answer, develop and justify lifestyle and nutritional guidance, and a fitness training programme for Mr Sharp, using the scenario in the task information, your preparatory notes and the lifestyle and health screening information.

Guided   **1**   Interpret the lifestyle factors and screening information for the selected individual.

> It's a good idea to produce a plan like the one below and use a checklist before tackling this question. Read the thought plan below, then complete the answer. The first part has been done for you.
>
> Mr Sharp: positive lifestyle factors: wants to start exercising.
>
> Negative lifestyle factors: no physical activity, unbalanced diet, consumes alcohol, smokes, minimum sleep, and work-related stress.
>
> Screening: positive results: resting heart rate (average).
>
> Negative results: blood pressure (pre-high BP), BMI (overweight), waist-to-hip ratio (high risk).

Mr Sharp's current lifestyle features several negative aspects which could lead to poor health and well-being. Positively, he wants to start incorporating more physical activity into his lifestyle, which will no doubt benefit his overall health. The first negative factor for Mr Sharp is that he does not partake in any physical activity; this can lead to both physical and psychological effects, including issues with weight which Mr Sharp already has. The second negative factor ....

....

....

....

....

....

....

....

Mr Sharp's resting heart rate is classified as average according to normative data for his age; this is a positive result for Mr Sharp's health and with increased participation in regular activity his resting heart rate should decrease further. ....

....

....

> Where possible refer to government recommendations or normative data. Your response must be **detailed**, **analytical** and **specifically relevant** to the client throughout.

> For more help with interpreting lifestyle factors and screening information revisit pages 44–48 and 87 of the Revision Guide.

Guided

2 Provide lifestyle modification techniques for the selected individual.

 For each lifestyle factor there are several possible modification techniques. Choose the most suitable for the client.

It's a good idea to produce a plan and use a checklist before tackling this question. Read the thought plan below, then complete the answer. The first part has been done for you.

Smoking: could start with self-help tips; use NHS stop-smoking services (free, accessible); use these resources before external help, e.g. NRT (costly, side effects).

Alcohol: could start with self-help tips to reduce alcohol at home and while out (simple lifestyle changes) – use these before external help (for excessive/prolonged drinking).

Physical activity: prioritise, manage daily routine, identify available time slots, incorporate into daily routine, undertake new leisure activities, and exercise with a friend.

Stress/sleep: an increase in exercise/an improved diet/less alcohol/no smoking can promote more sleep and help in managing stress.

Diet: use the Eat Well Plate to achieve a balanced diet; consider timing, number and choice of meals, hydration levels.

Screening results: blood pressure, BMI, WHR – modification with improved diet, exercise, reduction in alcohol and smoking.

Mr Sharp consumes 20 units of alcohol per week, which exceeds the government

recommendations. Reducing alcohol consumption is therefore a priority for Mr Sharp. There are

several strategies that Mr Sharp could try. Firstly, ...

....

....

....

....

....

....

....

....

Mr Sharp indicated in his screening form that on average he has 7 hours sleep per night. This is

only marginally below the recommendation of 8 hours, therefore this is not a priority for Mr Sharp.

However, he may find that changes to his lifestyle, including more exercise, less alcohol and a

balanced diet will positively affect his sleep routine. ....

....

....

Your lifestyle modification techniques must be **justified**, **prioritised** and be **specifically relevant** to the client's lifestyle and requirements.

Links For more help with providing lifestyle modification techniques revisit pages 44–52 and 88 of the Revision Guide.

3 Propose nutritional guidance for the selected individual.

> For nutritional guidance remember to consider fluid intake too.

 It's a good idea to produce a plan and use a checklist like the one below before tackling this question. Read the checklist then complete the answer. The first part has been done for you.

Diet: timing of meals, number of meals, food choices, avoid takeaways, healthier snacks, preparation/organisation, food labels, portion sizes, fluid intake.

Mr Sharp needs to make significant changes to his current diet to work towards achieving

a healthy body weight. One of the first areas for him to address is the fact that he misses

breakfast on a regular basis, which is ....

....

....

....

....

....

....

....

....

....

....

....

....

....

....

....

....

....

....

> Continue to propose nutritional advice for your client. Your nutritional guidance must be **justified** and **specifically relevant** to the client's dietary requirements.

> **Links** For more help with proposing nutritional guidance revisit pages 45, 58–64 and 89 of the Revision Guide.

Guided

4 Propose suitable training methods for the selected individual.

> Consider the most suitable training method for the client and their goal.

> It's a good idea to produce a plan and use a checklist like the one below before tackling this question. Read the checklist then complete the answer. The first part has been done for you.
>
> Training methods: individual's needs and aims, government recommendations, FITT principles.

Mr Sharp's training aims are towards taking part in 5-a-side football in 6 weeks' time. He currently does no exercise whatsoever so training needs to start off at a low intensity. I suggest

....

....

....

Fartlek training is a highly suitable method of training for Mr Sharp, particularly as it can be adapted to suit football by incorporating varying intensities and changes of direction, imitating a football match. This type of training is suitable for beginners like Mr Sharp as it can incorporate low, medium and high intensity. Fartlek training can be varied by ....

....

....

....

....

....

....

....

....

....

....

....

....

....

....

> Your proposals must be **justified** and be **specifically relevant** to the client's training requirements.

> For more help with proposing training methods revisit pages 44, 67–69, 81 and 90 of the Revision Guide.

Guided > 5 6-week training programme: design key stages (weeks 1, 3 and 6) of a 6-week training programme for the selected individual.

> 🖉 The notes for training programme design on pages 39–40 show examples of weeks 1, 3 and 6.
>
> Complete the programme below for Mr Sharp for an additional session for **week 6**.
>
> It's a good idea to produce a plan and use a checklist like the one below before tackling this question. Read the checklist and continue to answer the question.
>
> *Week 6: warm-up, main activity, cool-down, principles of training and FITT principles.*

	Sunday
Physical activity	Gym session
	Week 6 extra session:
	....
	....
	....
	....
	....
	Warm-up: jog 10 m, 10 times.
	Dynamic stretches to 10 m line and walking back: groin twists (ins and outs), lunges, side steps, high knee, bum kicks, sprints.
	Main activity: indoor fartlek training session:
	....
	....
	....
	....
	....
	....
	Cool-down:
	....

Your training programme must **demonstrate a thorough understanding** of the principles of training; this must be specifically **relevant** to the client's fitness/training/lifestyle requirements.

 For more help with designing a training programme revisit pages 65–79 and 91 of the Revision Guide.

6 Provide justification for the training programme that has been produced for the selected individual.

Ensure that you are able to **justify** the content of your training programme.

Guided

Produce a plan and use a checklist before tackling this question. Read the checklist to help you continue to answer the question below, then complete the answer. The first part has been done for you.

Justification: principles of training, FITT principles.

Mr Sharp's training programme focuses on developing aerobic fitness in preparation for him participating in 5-a-side football. Specifically, fartlek training has been included because

....

....

....

....

The frequency of Mr Sharp's sessions is progressive over the 6-week training programme.

Weeks 1 and 2 begin with two training sessions as Mr Sharp will not have participated in exercise

previous to this. In weeks 3 and 4 this is increased to three sessions per week, followed by four

sessions per week in weeks 5 and 6. ....

....

....

....

....

....

....

....

....

....

....

....

....

....

Your justification must **demonstrate a thorough understanding** of the principles of training and a **specific relevance** to the requirements of the client.

 Links For more help with producing justifications for training programmes revisit pages 80–83 and 92 of the Revision Guide.

Revision task 2

Reading the task information

Make sure you **read the task information thoroughly**. Perhaps read the scenario as a whole, then read it again and highlight key information about the client. Being clear on the task information from the outset will ensure that you fully understand your client and conduct the appropriate research and preparation for answering the questions.

Task information

Scenario

Miss Petts is a 40-year-old, full-time nurse, working a minimum of 37 hours per week. Her shifts start at 6 am and finish at 2 pm with a 45-minute lunch break. Her job involves being on her feet all day. She commutes the 2-mile journey to the hospital via car.

She feels that through the winter she has let her fitness decline, admitting that she is exercising less and less. She used to be a regular member of the gym's running club, 6 months ago. She has decided to enter the club's 10 K in 6 weeks' time. She currently exercises twice a week.

Miss Petts attends an annual fitness assessment. She is then given a 6-week training programme to follow.

Miss Petts has previously completed a PAR-Q and has indicated that she has no medical conditions and is fit to take part in activity.

Fill out the notes below, based on the task information above, to understand Miss Petts' key information.

1 Consider Miss Petts' age.

....

....

2 Write down key points relating to Miss Petts' occupation.

....

3 Consider whether exercise can be incorporated on the travel to and from work.

....

4 Are Miss Petts' lunch breaks an opportunity for incorporating exercise?

....

5 Consider Miss Petts' current physical fitness.

....

6 Consider Miss Petts' goal.

....

....

 Links For more help with reading the task information revisit page 85 of the Revision Guide.

Gathering information

Using preparatory notes

In this Revision Workbook you can refer to any of the notes you have made as you give answers to the questions (pages 64–70). Check with your tutor or look at the most up-to-date sample Assessment Material to see whether you can refer to your notes **in your actual assessment** or whether there are any restrictions on them.

Making notes on lifestyle factors and screening processes

 You will need to carry out preparatory work for the task and make notes. You will make use of these notes on lifestyle factors when responding to Question 1, on page 64. You could make notes using the headings below. Complete the notes below.

Miss Petts: positive lifestyle factors

Physical activity

....

....

Smoking

....

....

Alcohol

....

....

Stress

....

....

Sleep

....

....

Diet

....

....

Resting heart rate

	RESTING HEART RATE AGED 36–45
ATHLETE	
EXCELLENT	
GOOD	
ABOVE AVERAGE	
AVERAGE	
BELOW AVERAGE	
POOR	

BMI/waist-to-hip ratio

....

....

....

Blood pressure

....

....

....

Making notes on lifestyle modification techniques

> Complete the notes below to help you gather information and make notes on **lifestyle modification techniques**. You will make use of these notes when responding to Question 2, on page 65.

Physical activity

....
....
....
....

Smoking

....
....

Alcohol

....
....

Stress

....
....

Sleep

....
....

Diet

....
....
....
....

Resting heart rate

....
....

BMI/waist-to-hip ratio

....
....

Blood pressure

....
....

Making notes on nutritional guidance

> Complete the notes below to help you gather information and make notes on **nutritional guidance**. You will make use of these notes when responding to Question 3, on page 66.

Eat Well Plate

....
....
....
....
....
....
....
....
....
....

Strategies for Miss Petts

....
....
....
....
....
....
....
....
....
....

Fluid intake

....
....
....
....
....
....

Making notes on training methods

Complete the notes below to help you gather information and make notes on **training methods**. You will make use of these notes when responding to Question 4, on page 67.

Overview

....

....

....

Frequency

....

....

Intensity

....

....

Time

....

Type

....

....

Training method 1: continuous training

Advantages

....

....

....

Training method 2: core exercises

....

....

....

Miscellaneous

....

....

Making notes on designing a training programme

 Complete the notes below to help you gather information and make notes on **designing a training programme**. You will make use of these notes when responding to Question 5, on page 68.

Week 1

	Mon	Tues	Wed	Thurs	Fri	Sat	Sun
Physical activity							

Week 3

	Mon	Tues	Wed	Thurs	Fri	Sat	Sun
Physical activity							

Week 6

	Mon	Tues	Wed	Thurs	Fri	Sat	Sun
Physical activity							

Making notes on justifying your training programme

Complete the notes below to help you gather information and make notes on justifying your **training programme**. You will make use of these notes when responding to Question 6, on page 70.

Frequency

....

....

....

....

....

Intensity

....

....

....

....

....

Time

....

....

....

....

....

Type

....

....

....

....

....

Principles of training

....

....

....

....

....

Reviewing additional information

This additional information supports the task information. You will need to use both pieces of information to answer the questions.

Personal details

Section 1: Personal details

Name: **Miss Petts**
Address: **2 West View**
        Anytown
Home telephone: **01234 567890**
Mobile telephone: **07123456789**
Email: **m.petts@gmail.com**
Date of birth: **19/11/1976**
Please answer the following questions to the best of your knowledge.
Occupation
1. What is your occupation?
   Nurse
2. How many hours do you work weekly?
   37 hours – 6 am–2 pm 45-min lunch hour
3. How far do you live from your workplace?
   2 miles
4. How do you travel to work?
   Car

Current activity levels

Section 2: Current activity levels

1. How many times a week do you currently take part in physical activity?
   Attend the gym twice a week

Make sure you read the lifestyle questionnaire thoroughly and highlight key information about the client. Use this and your notes to interpret the needs of the individual in order to prepare guidance on lifestyle, nutrition and fitness training. Answer the questions below to help you.

 1 Consider how many sessions of physical activity per week you would recommend for Miss Petts.

....

....

 Links For more help with interpreting lifestyle questionnaires revisit page 53 of the Revision Guide.

Nutritional status

Section 3: Nutritional status

1. How many meals do you have each day? **3**

2. Do you take any supplements? If yes, which ones? **No**

Day 1	Breakfast	Lunch	Dinner	Snacks
Y/N	Y	Y	Y	Y
Time of day	6.00 am	11.30 am	6 pm	Mid-morning Mid-afternoon Evening
Food intake	Porridge	Ham and cheese panini	Fish and chips	Banana Crisps Chocolate
Fluid intake	4 x coffees, 1 bottle of water, can of fizzy drink, 1 glass of wine			
Day 2	Breakfast	Lunch	Dinner	Snacks
Y/N	Y	Y	Y	Y
Time of day	6.00 am	11.30 am	6 pm	Mid-morning Mid-afternoon Evening
Food intake	Porridge	Cheese and tomato toastie with potato wedges	Pizza and salad	Apple Crisps Cheese and biscuits
Fluid intake	4 x coffees, 1 bottle of water, can of fizzy drink, 2 glasses of wine			

When interpreting the client's nutritional intake, remember to consider the following aspects: the Eat Well Plate/food choices, fluid intake, timing and number of meals, portion sizes, organisation and preparation, training needs. Answer the questions below to help you.

1 Looking at **day 1**, what are the key issues with Miss Petts' eating and drinking habits?

....

....

2 Looking at **day 2**, what are the key issues with Miss Petts' eating and drinking habits?

....

....

Links For more help with providing nutritional guidance revisit pages 58–64 and 89 of the Revision Guide.

Your lifestyle

Section 4: Your lifestyle

Please answer the following questions to the best of your knowledge.
1. How many units of alcohol do you drink in a typical week? **15**
2. Do you smoke? **Yes** If yes, how many a day? **5**
3. Do you experience stress on a daily basis? **No**
4. If yes, what causes you stress (if you know)? **N/A**
5. On average, how many hours sleep do you get per night? **6**

Health monitoring tests – test results

Section 5: Health monitoring tests – test results

Test	Result
Blood pressure	115/77 mmHg
Resting heart rate	74 bpm
Body mass index	25
Waist-to-hip-ratio	0.83

Physical activity/sporting goals

Section 6: Physical activity/sporting goals

1. What are your physical activity/sporting goals?

   To complete a 10K in 6 weeks

CLIENT DECLARATION

I have understood and answered all of the above questions honestly.

Signed Client: **M.Petts**   Print Name: **Mary Petts**   Date: **05/05/16**

When interpreting your individual's lifestyle factors, think about their smoking habits, alcohol consumption, diet, physical activity, stress, sleep and health monitoring results. You are establishing their strengths, areas for improvement and, where possible, comparing their responses/results to government recommendations, guidelines and normative data. Answer the questions below to help you.

1   Miss Petts has indicated that she consumes **15** units of alcohol per week. Interpret this response.

....

....

2   Miss Petts' BMI has measured at **25**. Interpret this result.

....

....

Links   For more help with interpreting lifestyle factors revisit pages 44–52 of the Revision Guide. For interpreting the results of health monitoring tests revisit pages 54–57 of the Revision Guide.

Questions

All questions relate to the task brief featuring Miss Petts. Answer all questions.

1   Interpret the lifestyle factors and screening information for the selected individual.

It's a good idea to produce a plan and use a checklist before tackling this question.

....
....
....
....
....
....
....
....
....
....
....
....
....
....
....
....
....
....
....
....
....
....
....
....

Your response must be **detailed, analytical and specifically relevant** to the client's lifestyle throughout. Remember to refer to the screening information provided.

Links For help with interpreting lifestyle factors revisit pages 44–48 and 87 of the Revision Guide.

2 Provide lifestyle modification techniques for the selected individual.

> For each lifestyle factor there are several possible modification techniques. Remember to choose the most suitable for the client and their lifestyle.
>
> It's a good idea to produce a plan and use a checklist before tackling this question.

....

....

....

....

....

....

....

....

....

....

....

....

....

....

....

....

....

....

....

....

....

> Your lifestyle modification techniques must be **justified, prioritised and be specifically relevant** to the individual's lifestyle and requirements. Consider why you have chosen these techniques for this client.

> **Links** For help with providing lifestyle modification techniques, revisit pages 44–52 and 88 of the Revision Guide.

3 Provide nutritional guidance for the selected individual.

> For nutritional guidance remember to consider fluid intake too.
>
> It's a good idea to produce a plan and use a checklist before tackling this question.

....

....

....

....

....

....

....

....

....

....

....

....

....

....

....

....

....

....

....

....

....

....

> Your nutritional guidance must be **justified and specifically relevant** to the client's dietary requirements. Consider justifying using the Eat Well Plate and the sport the individual is training for.

> **Links** For help with providing nutritional guidance revisit pages 45, 68–64 and 89 of the Revision Guide.

4 Propose suitable training methods for the selected individual.

> Consider the most suitable training method for the client and their training needs and goal.
>
> It's a good idea to produce a plan and use a checklist before tackling this question.

....

....

....

....

....

....

....

....

....

....

....

....

....

....

....

....

....

....

....

....

....

....

> Your proposals must be **justified and be specifically relevant** to the client's training requirements. Consider their level of fitness and sport.

> **Links** For help with proposing suitable training methods revisit pages 44, 68–71, 81 and 90 of the Revision Guide.

5 6-week training programme: design key stages (weeks 1, 3 and 6) of a 6-week training programme for the selected individual.

 Design weeks 1, 3 and 6 of a 6-week training programme for Miss Petts. Ensure that you fully consider and incorporate the FITT principles and the principles of training throughout all weeks.

It's a good idea to produce a plan and use a checklist before tackling this question.

Week 1

	Mon	Tues	Wed	Thurs	Fri	Sat	Sun
Physical activity							

Ensure that you are now fully considering and incorporating the **FITT principles** and the **principles of training**, particularly **progression**. Ensure that you do not lose focus on what your client's aims are.

Week 3

	Mon	Tues	Wed	Thurs	Fri	Sat	Sun
Physical activity							

Your client is near the end of their 6-week training programme. Ensure that you are preparing them fully to achieve their aim.

Week 6

	Mon	Tues	Wed	Thurs	Fri	Sat	Sun
Physical activity							

Your training programme must demonstrate a **thorough understanding of the principles of training**. This must be **specifically relevant** to the client's fitness/training/lifestyle requirements.

 Links For help with designing a training programme revisit pages 65–79 and 91 of the Revision Guide.

6 Provide justification for the training programme that has been produced for the selected individual.

> ✏️ Ensure that you are able to justify the content of your training programme, explaining how and why you incorporated the FITT principles and principles of training.
>
> It's a good idea to produce a plan and use a checklist before tackling this question.

....

....

....

....

....

....

....

....

....

....

....

....

....

....

....

....

....

....

....

....

....

....

....

> Your justification must demonstrate a **thorough understanding of the principles of training** and be of **specific relevance** to the training requirements of the individual.

> 🔗 **Links** For help with producing justifications for training programmes, revisit pages 80–83 and 92 of the Revision Guide.

Answers

Unit 1: Anatomy and Physiology

Revision test 1 (guided)

Section A: Skeletal system for sports performance (page 2)

1 (a) Flat bone **(1)**

(b) Its function is to provide protection **(1)**. It achieves this by forming a hard shell around the brain **(1)**, absorbing the impact of the fall, avoiding a worse injury to the brain, such as concussion or brain damage **(1)**.

2 Regular exercise will cause the body to adapt. The regular increase in mineral uptake will increase the strength of the bone **(1)**, therefore reducing the risk of osteoporosis **(1)**.

3 The shoulder joint is a ball and socket joint. The joint is formed by the meeting of the humerus and scapula. The humerus forms the 'ball' in the joint, allowing the bone to move in many different directions. These types of joints have the greatest range of movement. For example, in the picture we can see the bowler has rotated the arm at the shoulder. The humerus is a long bone and therefore provides leverage. This means the bowler can deliver the ball with speed: the faster the bowl, the harder it will be to hit. Long bones are also involved in red blood cell production, therefore ensuring there are sufficient red blood cells for oxygen delivery. The scapula is a flat bone and therefore offers protection. All of these features make it possible for the bowler to carry out the technique of bowling. If the bowler's range of movement were limited, he would be unable to perform the technique correctly. For example, if he were unable to rotate the arm completely, the bowl would be more of a throw and therefore an illegal bowl, or it would make it more difficult to aim accurately at the stumps, increasing the risk of bowling a wide ball and giving away unnecessary runs. **(6)**

Section B: Muscular system for sports performance (page 4)

4 Two characteristics of cardiac muscle are: 1. It is non-fatiguing muscle **(1)**. This makes it ideal for its function, as it is essential the heart continues to beat throughout life without taking a rest **(1)**. 2. It is an involuntary muscle **(1)**. This means we do not have to think consciously to make the heart beat, so we can concentrate on other things such as tactics or how to perform a technique **(1)**.

5 The hip flexors work as the agonist muscle in this movement, as they contract to flex the hip **(1)**, but they can only contract if the gluteals work antagonistically with them, relaxing to allow hip flexion **(1)**.

6 Athlete 2 may have a higher percentage of type IIx/fast twitch muscle fibres **(1)**. Therefore, she could generate more power, allowing her to jump higher **(1)**. In addition, this athlete may have carried out more relevant training **(1)** so the adaptations to the muscular system are greater **(1)**.

7 There are three different types of muscle contraction: isometric, concentric and eccentric. During the squat there are three distinct phases of movement. At first, Sam moves downward lowering the weight into the squat position by bending her legs at the knee and flexing the hip. During this phase the quadriceps contract eccentrically; this means they are lengthening but are still contracting to produce the required force to control the rate of descent of the body with the additional weight. At the end of the downward phase the body is stationary, the muscles are still working to maintain the body position and the weight of the barbell but as there is no movement they are working isometrically. Finally, during the upwards phase the quadriceps contract concentrically, shortening to provide the force needed to lift the weight as Sam stands up. Without the ability to use different types of muscle contractions for the different phases

of the movement Sam would not be able to complete the technique. **(6)**

Section C: The respiratory system for sports performance (page 7)

8 (a) A = tidal volume **(1)**, B = vital capacity **(1)**.

(b) The trace for tidal volume is very even. This would suggest that these readings were taken when Heather was at rest **(1)** because exercise at varying intensities will cause the breathing rate to fluctuate **(1)**. This would be shown on the graph by tidal volume traces being closer together when breathing at a faster rate. The traces could also change height if depth of breathing altered **(1)**.

9 (a) To monitor carbon dioxide **(1)** and pH levels of blood **(1)**.

(b) The medulla oblongata transfers messages to and from the spinal cord and the brain **(1)** to control the action of the diaphragm and intercostal muscles **(1)**. By varying the speed of the impulses from the medulla oblongata to the diaphragm and external intercostal muscles, breathing rate can be increased or decreased depending on the level of intensity of the activity **(1)**.

10 As the cyclists are competing in a long-distance event, they will need a continuous supply of oxygen for energy production so they can continue to cycle. Therefore, during exercise the rate of gaseous exchange increases to try to meet the increased oxygen demand as well as the increased need to remove carbon dioxide that is being produced by the body. However, at high altitude the partial pressure of oxygen is lower, so there will be less oxygen available in the air breathed in for the cyclists to extract and transport to the muscles. As the partial pressure of oxygen drops the amount of oxygen carried by the haemoglobin in red blood cells also drops. This means that the body will be less efficient at removing waste. This can reduce the efficiency of the energy systems, reducing energy available to the cyclists. With less oxygen available the body cannot work at the same level of intensity. Therefore, performance levels will drop as the cyclists will experience muscle fatigue more rapidly. To conclude, owing to the lower partial pressure of oxygen at altitude, and the cyclists' increased need for oxygen transport due to the intensity of the exercise they are performing, working at high altitude will make it harder for them to maintain the quality of their performance. Therefore, they will not be able to cycle as well at high altitude as they could at sea level. **(6)**

Section D: The cardiovascular system for sports performance (page 10)

11 (a) Another role of the cardiovascular system during exercise is thermoregulation **(1)** by vasoconstriction and vasodilation **(1)** of blood vessels. This is because during exercise our temperature increases, and if left unchecked could increase core temperature **(1)**, which would make it difficult to continue. Therefore, we need to increase blood flow to the capillaries near the surface of the skin to lose heat **(1)**.

(b) (i)

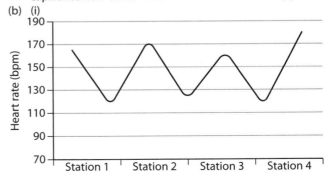

(2)

(ii) Immediately after the exercise there should be a steep drop in heart rate at first **(1)**, although this will gradually level out, becoming less steep as the recovery period goes on. Heart rate will still drop, but more slowly **(1)**.

(c) The sinoatrial node acts as a pacemaker, controlling how quickly the heart contracts **(1)**. It initiates the heartbeat by sending electrical impulses, causing the atria to contract **(1)**. This impulse is passed to the ventricles and the Purkinje fibres signal both ventricles to contract **(1)**. Therefore, by controlling the rate that these electrical impulses are sent, heart rate is controlled. The sympathetic nervous system sends messages to increase heart rate during exercise **(1)**. The parasympathetic nervous system sends messages to the sinoatrial node to reduce heart rate during less intense exercise **(1)**.

12 Veins return blood to the heart **(1)**. However, the blood in veins is under low pressure **(1)**, therefore veins need valves to prevent the backflow of blood, so the blood continues to move back towards the heart **(1)**.

13 A medical check is carried out by the organisers of the fitness class to check to see if Benji has any pre-existing medical conditions such as high blood pressure, which could impact how hard he should train. As Benji is not used to strenuous activity, he doesn't know if he is healthy enough to take part in the class. Without these medical checks he may attempt training at too high a level making any health condition worse, or triggering another condition. For example, if Benji has high blood pressure, as he exercises his blood pressure will increase further in response to the exercise, especially if it is a weight training class. This could increase his blood pressure to a dangerous level, resulting in stroke or heart attack. The fitness centre would also need to check Benji's family history for heart disease, such as SADS. This is a hereditary disease, so Benji may also have this condition, and owing to the limited side effects he may not even be aware he has it.

Although for most people medical screening does not show any health conditions that the organisers and individual need to be aware of, for those with an existing cardiovascular health condition medical screening is essential as, rather than improve health through regular exercise, the individual is running the risk of making their health worse, and in extreme cases, such as with SADS, they run the risk of sudden death. **(6)**

Section E: Energy systems for sports performance (page 13)

14 (a) ATP is resynthesised through anaerobic glycolysis **(1)**. Glucose is broken down **(1)** to form pyruvate **(1)** and two additional molecules of ATP **(1)**.

(b) The lactate system can only be used for a limited amount of time because the waste products of anaerobic glycolysis, such as lactate **(1)**, increase the acidity of the blood **(1)**, making it more difficult to continue with energy production, causing muscle fatigue **(1)**.

15 Endurance athletes with diabetes have to monitor their blood glucose levels, to make sure they are high enough to allow participation in events that take a long time to complete **(1)**. Based on their blood glucose levels they may need to eat carbohydrates before, during and after their activity to balance their glucose levels and prevent a hypoglycaemic attack **(1)**. If they are unable to maintain the right energy levels throughout the event, their performance will be worse, their times will be slower or they may even need to pull out of the event **(1)**.

16 There are three energy systems that will be used at varying times throughout a long-distance race, so if any adapt this should be advantageous to the runner. For example, at the end of the race is a 'sprint finish'. If the ATP-PC system adapted, there would be increased creatine stores so the runner could accelerate for longer to either increase the lead over an opponent or catch them up if they were in the lead. This is because stores of PC would increase, allowing greater resynthesis of ATP for energy production, so that the use of this system could be extended for a further 1 or 2 seconds. Similarly, if the lactate system adapted by increasing its tolerance to lactate, the muscles would not experience fatigue as quickly, allowing the runners to run a faster lap when needed, although this pace could not be maintained throughout the race without time for recovery. Adaptations to the aerobic system would mean the runner would be able to utilise fat stores more easily as an energy source. This would provide unlimited stores of energy so they could continue to work throughout the race. They would also have increased glycogen stores and mitochondria, increasing energy available and the number of sites in the muscle for aerobic respiration; all contributing to a continuous supply of energy over the course of the 25 laps.

Therefore, although adaptations to each energy system can be advantageous to the long-distance runner, the most significant adaptations in terms of performance are on the aerobic energy system, due to the time taken to complete the race. **(6)**

Section F: Interrelationships between body systems for sports performance (page 15)

17 The muscular system allows us to move to play sport or take part in exercise. This is because muscles are arranged in antagonistic pairs: when one muscle contracts, the other relaxes so that movement is possible. However, in order to contract, the muscle first requires energy.

The role of the cardiovascular system is to transport oxygen and nutrients to the muscle, and to remove waste products such as carbon dioxide and lactate. The oxygen is used in energy production within the muscle, which can be used to maintain performance at the time, or in quieter parts of the game to recover anaerobic energy and oxygen stores in the muscle so they are ready 'to go again' – without this, performers would not be able to continue to chase through balls, hit powerful shots on goal, or gain height to head the ball clear. To last for 90 minutes the supply of food fuel sources and oxygen must be constant. Also, the removal of waste products is essential so that the acidity of the blood does not increase, reducing the efficiency of the muscles in energy production. Although there is enough stored energy in the muscles for 1 or 2 seconds of exercise, after this the muscles are reliant on the cardiovascular system fulfilling its role to ensure adequate energy production for physical activity, and the cardiovascular system relies on the contractions of the muscles to help the return of the blood to the heart through the veins. If the systems did not work together it would be impossible to participate in sport and exercise. **(8)**

Revision test 2

Section A: Skeletal system for sports performance (page 16)

1 (a) A = articular cartilage **(1)**, B = bursa **(1)**.

(b) C = the ligaments **(1)**. Their function is to join bone to bone **(1)**. This is important to a sports performer as, provided the ligaments are strong enough, they will stop the joint dislocating **(1)**. For example, if the performer has to twist quickly to swerve past an opponent, the knee should not dislocate **(1)**.

2 Cartilaginous joints in the upper skeleton are the cervical and thoracic vertebrae. In the lower skeleton, they are lumbar vertebrae. These vertebrae are irregular in shape and have discs of cartilage between them. The discs of cartilage allow the joints to be slightly moveable, so there is a limited amount of movement between each vertebra and the vertebrae next to it. However, given the number of vertebrae, the small amount of movement between each one becomes a large range of movement when considering the movement from the first cervical vertebrae to the last lumber vertebrae. This means that the performer is able to bend their back to create an arch shape. We can see this arch shape in the picture. The jumper's back is arched so she can get as close to the bar as possible without knocking the bar off. If she were unable to form this arch, she would need to jump higher; making it harder to clear the bar as she would need to lift her whole body above the bar, rather than just a part of the body (head and shoulders, hips, knees and ankles). **(6)**

Section B: Muscular system for sports performance (page 18)

3 (a) The athlete's muscle contracts suddenly and powerfully **(1)** and is very painful **(1)**.

(b) The athlete should make sure they stretch/warm up thoroughly before the activity **(1)**.

4 (a) To begin with, the leg is flexed at the knee and dorsiflexed at the ankle **(1)**. The gastrocnemius contracts **(1)** while the tibialis anterior relaxes to plantarflex the foot at the ankle **(1)**. The quadriceps are able to contract as the hamstrings relax, allowing the swimmer to extend the leg at the knee **(1)**.

(b) Type IIx **(1)**, as these fibres tend to be thicker and larger than other fibre types, so can produce a stronger force of contraction **(1)**, which the swimmers need for an explosive and powerful start to the race to give them vital tenths of a second advantage **(1)**.

5 The muscular system adaptations include hypertrophy of the muscle fibres, an increase in myoglobin stores, increased tolerance to lactate and an increase in tendon strength. While all of these adaptations will contribute to increased fitness for basketball, some could have a bigger impact than others. Some of the adaptations are aerobic, while others are anaerobic, so they will each be relevant to different parts of the game. In the picture, Jacob has jumped high to get closer to the basket to increase his chance of scoring. This will be possible due to muscular hypertrophy of his type II muscle fibres. By increasing the muscle size, he is able to exert more force into the ground to push him higher into the air. This is a great advantage when shooting and also when defending, blocking opponents' shots or if trying to intercept a high pass. Adaptation of his fast twitch muscle fibres will also increase his ability to accelerate on the court, allowing fast breaks and increasing the opportunity to have a clear shot at the basket. However, these adaptations will have limited use without other adaptations. For example, without an efficient recovery process Jacob will get too tired on court to carry out these actions. Therefore, the increase in myoglobin is also important as this provides an oxygen store for the muscles so they can recover during less intense moments of the game, such as during a time-out, or if an opponent has a free throw. **(6)**

Section C: The respiratory system for sports performance (page 21)

6 (a) From the trachea, the air enters the bronchus **(1)** and then the bronchioles in the lungs **(1)**. The bronchioles have alveoli at the ends **(1)**. These are surrounded by capillaries ready to take the oxygen from the air to the rest of the body **(1)**.

(b) During inspiration, the diaphragm and external intercostal muscles contract **(1)** so that the area inside the thoracic cavity is increased, allowing the lungs to expand **(1)**. This means that the pressure within the lungs drops compared to outside, causing air to enter the lungs **(1)**.

7 (a) Vital capacity is the volume of air that can be inspired or expired per breath, including forced breathing **(1)**.

(b) Residual volume **(1)**.

(c) Increased vital capacity means carbon dioxide can be expelled from the body more rapidly **(1)**.

8 Gaseous exchange is the movement of oxygen into the body and the movement of carbon dioxide out of the body. It takes place between the alveoli and blood stream in the lungs and between the tissues and the blood stream in the muscles. Oxygen from the air enters the alveoli in the lungs. This increases the oxygen concentration in the alveolus compared to the low concentration in the capillary. This is low as the oxygen has been used by the triathlete in energy production for their event. The oxygen diffuses from the alveolus into the capillary owing to the difference in concentration. Carbon dioxide moves in the opposite direction because levels are high in the blood as it is produced during the race and lower in the alveolus. When the triathletes are racing, the respiratory system responds by increasing breathing rate and tidal volume. This happens so that more air, containing oxygen, can be breathed in and also so that carbon dioxide removal can keep up with its production during the race. An increase in tidal volume will increase the amount of air in each breath, making sure there is a high difference in oxygen concentration. Similarly, breathing rate increases, speeding up the movement of air into and out of the lungs. This increase in rate and depth of breathing experienced by the triathlete speeds up diffusion rates so that the exchange of gases occurs more quickly, providing these athletes with the oxygen that is essential for them to maintain the quality of their performance over each stage of the race, and therefore their overall race time. Without this increase in gaseous exchange, oxygen levels would be reduced, so there would be less energy available for the race, forcing the triathlete to slow down. **(6)**

Section D: The cardiovascular system for sports performance (page 23)

9 (a) A = septum **(1)**, B = vena cava **(1)**.

(b) C = semi-lunar valve **(1)**. Its function is to prevent the back flow of blood into the heart **(1)**. This is important to a sports performer because if this happened there would be less blood available to carry oxygen to the muscles **(1)**, leading to a potential lack of oxygen for energy production, so performance levels would drop **(1)**.

(c) This is achieved through an anticipatory rise **(1)**. This is where the heart rate increases just before exercise, therefore ensuring increased oxygen delivery to the performer **(1)**. It is caused by an increase in adrenaline **(1)**.

10 (a) Segment B shows the percentage of blood flow to the skin during exercise **(1)**. Blood flow to the skin needs to be higher during exercise to help with heat loss **(1)** as more heat is generated during exercise than at rest **(1)**.

(b) Smooth muscle **(1)** in the walls of the arterioles supplying the skin **(1)** relaxes to allow the vessel to vasodilate to increase blood flow to this area **(1)**.

(c) The performer would overheat, so they would not be able to work at their optimum level **(1)**.

11 The capillaries' role is to allow gaseous exchange between the blood stream and the tissues. In order for this process to happen, the blood will need to travel at a slow speed so there is time for diffusion to take place, otherwise the person exercising will not be able to extract enough oxygen from the blood. The blood vessel that shows the slowest speed is C, so this must represent the capillary.

Arteries carry blood away from the heart and are responsible for ensuring that the blood is moved from the heart to the rest of the body. They are the closest vessels to the heart and therefore influenced the most by the heart contractions. Fluctuations in the velocity of the blood are most obvious in column A. These fluctuations link to the contraction and relaxation of the heart, therefore, as the arteries are closest to the heart, A represents the arteries. As the arterioles link the arteries and capillaries, B must be the arterioles. This is supported on the graph by a gradual dropping in the velocity of the blood. Columns D and E show a gradual increase in the velocity of the blood, but a constant lowering of blood pressure. As the blood moves further from the heart, blood pressure drops. Blood pressure in the veins is very low. This is why after exercise it is important to cool down, so that the action of the muscles can assist with the return of blood to the heart by massaging the blood vessels. This is also why veins have valves, so the type of blood vessel at the lowest pressure in column E must be the veins. Column D represents the venules, which form the link between the capillaries and the veins. **(6)**

Section E: Energy systems for sports performance (page 26)

12 (a) Phosphocreatine **(1)**.
   (b) The chemical bond between the phosphate and creatine molecule breaks, releasing energy that is then used to resynthesise ATP **(1)**.
13 Because of a lack of oxygen **(1)**, pyruvate cannot be broken down **(1)** so forms lactate **(1)**.
14 Aerobic **(1)**.
15 Although the body has large stores of fat, these are slow to break down **(1)**. Carbohydrates are a much quicker source to break down, but there are limited supplies in the body **(1)**. Therefore, the cyclists need to supplement these stores when racing so they have sufficient carbohydrate to complete the race **(1)**. Otherwise they would need to rely on fat stores, which would mean they would need to slow down **(1)**.
16 The 400 m runner will gain energy to explode from the blocks from the ATP-PC system. This energy system allows the muscles to generate a great deal of power quickly and, therefore, is vital at the start of the race as these powerful muscular contractions will allow the runner to accelerate in the first few metres of the race. At the same time that the ATP-PC system begins energy production, so too will the lactate system. This takes slightly longer to produce energy than the ATP-PC system, so it will not be used as much at the start of the race. However, the ATP-PC system only has sufficient stores of PC to provide energy for approximately 10 seconds before needing to recover. As the 400 m race is so short and run at such a high intensity, there is no time to recover this system during the race. The bulk of the energy produced for the remainder of the 400 m race will therefore be from the lactate energy system. This still produces energy quickly, which means the runner can run at a fast speed. The aerobic system does contribute to energy production, but this is a small amount compared to the other systems as the process of energy production is longer. It is mainly involved in the recovery processes after the race, as lactate will need breaking down and PC stores will need reforming. Therefore, although the aerobic energy system contributes to the recovery process after the race, the most significant contributions during the race are made by the ATP-PC and lactate energy systems. **(6)**

Section F: Interrelationships between body systems for sports performance (page 29)

17 The respiratory system adapts to regular aerobic training by increasing the strength of the respiratory muscles so that they can contract with more force, so that a greater volume of air can be taken into the lungs. Vital capacity is also increased and there is an increase in the rate of gaseous exchange due to adaptations to the cardiovascular system. The aerobic energy system also undergoes adaptations. For example, it is better able to utilise fat stores for energy production; there is an increased storage of glycogen in the muscle; and there are more mitochondria. Although the respiratory system does adapt to regular training, the intake of air is not thought to limit ability in endurance events. Therefore, even if the respiratory system did not adapt, it is likely that sufficient air would be inhaled in each breath to allow diffusion of enough oxygen into the mitochondria in the muscles. The more critical adaptation would be that, with the increased number of mitochondria, sufficient energy would still be provided by aerobic respiration. In contrast, if the aerobic energy system failed to adapt, this would mean fewer mitochondria, and therefore less opportunity for aerobic energy production. This would impact far more on energy production and would have a more detrimental effect on performance, as without appropriate energy levels the performer could not work as hard or for as long, therefore increasing the time taken to complete the race. This would also impact on their training, limiting the amount of work they could do and, therefore, future training adaptations. **(8)**

Unit 2: Fitness Training and Programming for Health, Sport and Well-being

Revision task 1 (guided)

Reading the task information (page 32)

2 • Works 8.30 am–3.30 pm.
  • Meetings at lunch.
  • Teacher – not necessarily an active profession.
  • Only 45 min for lunch.
4 Meetings at lunch – not long enough period to get changed, exercise and re-changed. Possible opportunity to have a walk.
5 • Doesn't currently exercise at all.
  • Exercise needs to be appropriate for a beginner.

Gathering information
Making notes on lifestyle factors and screening processes (page 33)

To complete the answer, include the following suggested points.
Physical activity
• Physical – reduces risk of chronic diseases, improves body shape, weight control.
• Psychological – improves mood/self-esteem, concentration, relieves stress and depression.
Smoking
• Choose five from the following: breathe more easily, more energy, improves smell and taste, less stress, improves fertility, better sex, younger looking skin, whiter teeth and fresher breath, live longer, protect loved ones.
Alcohol
• Government recommends 14 units.
• Long-term effects: brain damage, cancer, heart attack.
Stress
• Long-term effects: poor immune system, heart disease, stroke, hypertension, diabetes, skin conditions, angina, stomach ulcers.

Sleep

- Recommendation is 8 hours per night.
- Effects of poor sleep: poor immune system, heart disease, diabetes, stress, high blood pressure.

Diet

- Benefits of a healthy diet: improves immune function, increases energy, prevents disease, maintains weight, improves mood.

BMI

- 18.5–24.9 = healthy weight

Waist-to-hip ratio

- 0.96–1.0 = moderate risk

Resting heart rate

- Athlete 49–54
- Excellent 55–61
- Good 62–65

Blood pressure

- Risks associated with high BP: strain on heart, strain on blood vessels, risk of heart attack, risk of stroke, kidney disease, vascular disease.

Making notes on lifestyle modification techniques (page 35)

To complete the answer, include the following suggested points.

Physical activity

- Strength training – twice per week.
- Strategies to overcome the cost barrier: choose activities that are free, exercise at home.
- Strategies to overcome the lack of energy/motivation: plan ahead with exercise, think positively, invite a friend, exercise in the morning to avoid excuses, ensure variety, set achievable goals.

Alcohol

- Tips for reducing drinking at home: drink with food, avoid stocking up, distract yourself.

Sleep

- Recommended amount: 8 hours.

Diet

- Consider the timing of meals.
- Consider fluid intake.

BMI/WHR

- Increasing activity.

Making notes on nutritional guidance (page 37)

To complete the answer, include the following suggested points.

Eat Well Plate

- Some milk and dairy: through cereal for breakfast, yoghurts, etc.

Strategies for Mr Sharp

- Number of meals: does Mr Sharp miss any meals? If he does, he needs to be encouraged not to miss any and instead opt for a healthy option.
- Be better prepared and organised – snacks and meals could be prepared and a menu set for the week.

Fluid intake

- Consider fluid intake for Mr Sharp. Does he achieve the 2–2.5 litres per day? May need to increase when exercising.
- Caffeine needs to be in moderation. Maximum recommendation is 4–5 cups per day. It could be beneficial to reduce caffeine intake.

Making notes on training methods (page 38)

To complete the answer, include the following suggested points.

Frequency

- Begin with two/three training sessions per week as a beginner and increase over the 6-week period.

Intensity

- Low intensity to begin with: 50–60% heart-rate training zone.

Type

- Goal is to partake in football, so activities need to mimic the sport with more running-based activities.

Interval training advantages

- Replicates team games.
- Can be easier to check if the athlete is trying.

Circuit training advantages

- Less boring as changes all the time.
- Easily adapted for strength/endurance.
- Easily adapted for different sports.

Making notes on designing a training programme (page 39)

To complete the answer, include the following suggested points.

Monday

- Warm-up: 5-min fast walk.
- Cool-down: 5-min walk, reducing pace each minute.

Wednesday

- Flexibility section: static stretches held for 6 sec, then repeated for 8 sec – quads, calves, hamstrings, hips, back, stomach.

Making notes on justifying your training programme (page 41)

To complete the answer, include the following suggested points.

Type

- Flexibility and strength – specifically concentrating on lower body muscles – muscles required for football.

Principles of training

- Rest and recuperation – always two rest days to allow for growth and repair.
- Progression – in activities over the 6 weeks: factors are manipulated to ensure progression, e.g. sets, heart rate and time.
- Variation – the sessions are varied and include different activities, to avoid boredom.

Reviewing additional information Current activity levels (page 42)

1. Beginner, so start with 2–3 sessions per week and gradually increase frequency.

Nutritional status (page 43)

2. No breakfast, limited fruit and no vegetables, biscuits, not achieving recommended hydration levels, alcohol intake (if continued for rest of week) could be above recommendations, takeaway.

Physical activity/sporting goals (page 45)

1.
   - 20 units is above government recommendations for alcohol intake per week.
   - It will negatively affect the body (short- and long-term effects) and training.
2.
   - 135/88 mmHg is interpreted as pre-high blood pressure.
   - If this continues to develop to high blood pressure it could cause significant health risks.

Questions (page 46)

1. To complete the answer, include the following suggested points.

   Mr Sharp's current lifestyle features several negative aspects which could lead to poor health and well-being. Positively, he wants to start incorporating more physical activity into his lifestyle, which will no doubt benefit his overall health. The first negative factor for Mr Sharp is that he does not partake in any physical activity; this can lead to both physical and psychological effects, including issues with weight which Mr Sharp already has.

   - More exercise may reduce Mr Sharp's weight/BMI/WHR, may reduce stress and help sleep more.

   Negative factor – **unbalanced diet** – missing meals/limited food groups/limited hydration.

   - Not achieving government recommendations/guidelines for diet.
   - Negative effects of an unbalanced diet on health and well-being, e.g. poor immune system, weight increase, can impair mood.

- An improved diet may reduce Mr Sharp's weight/BMI/WHR, may improve stress.

Negative factor – **alcohol consumption** – drinks 20 units per week
- Exceeds government recommendations for alcohol consumption, which is 14 units.
- Negative effects of alcohol, e.g. short-/long-term effects, mental health problems.
- Less alcohol may reduce Mr Sharp's weight/BMI/WHR, may reduce stress and help him sleep better, and may reduce number of cigarettes smoked as may be consumed together.

Negative factor – **smoking** – 10 per day
- Negative effects of smoking, e.g. lung-, heart- and other health-related conditions.
- Quitting smoking may allow Mr Sharp to breath more easily when exercising.

Negative factor – **lack of sleep** – 7 hours per night
- Negative effects of lack of sleep, e.g. stress/high blood pressure.
- More sleep may reduce Mr Sharp's stress and lower blood pressure.

Negative factor – **stress** – school deadlines
- Negative effects of stress, e.g. heart disease/stomach ulcers.
- Less stress may reduce alcohol/smoking/blood pressure.

Mr Sharp's resting heart rate is classified as average according to normative data for his age; this is a positive result for Mr Sharp's health and with increased participation in regular activity his resting heart rate should decrease further.

However a negative factor – **blood pressure** – classified as pre-high blood pressure.
- Risks associated with high blood pressure, e.g. heart disease/heart attack.
- Increased exercise/improved diet/less alcohol/less stress will improve BP.

Negative factor – **BMI** – classified as overweight.
- Risks associated with high BMI, e.g. hypertension, cardiovascular disease, diabetes.
- Increased exercise/improved diet/less alcohol will improve BMI.

Negative factor – **waist-to-hip ratio** – classified as high risk.
- Risks associated with high WHR, e.g. increased risk of certain diseases.
- Increased exercise/improved diet/less alcohol will improve WHR.

2 To complete the answer, include the following suggested points.

Mr Sharp consumes 20 units of alcohol per week, which exceeds the government recommendations. Reducing alcohol consumption is therefore a priority for Mr Sharp. There are several strategies that Mr Sharp could try. Firstly…

Alcohol – recommendations are for Mr Sharp to reduce alcohol intake first to below the government recommendations, and then to further reduce intake to be able to lose weight, be healthier and be more able to participate in football effectively.
- Strategies for Mr Sharp to reduce alcohol intake: to start with self-help tips, as well as an improvement in diet/exercise/smoking; these may mean he naturally stops drinking as much.
- Strategies for Mr Sharp to reduce alcohol at home: drink with food, void stocking up with alcohol, keep distracted.
- Strategies for Mr Sharp to reduce alcohol while out: set a drinking limit, opt out of rounds and budget a fixed amount to spend on drinking.
- If the above methods are ineffective and his drinking becomes an issue, he could try external help, but at this stage this is not necessary.

Smoking – recommend that Mr Sharp give up smoking.
- Strategies for Mr Sharp to quit: start with self-help tips, as well as an improvement in diet/drinking/exercise; these may mean he naturally stops smoking or smokes less.
- If the above methods are ineffective he could seek support from the NHS stop-smoking service, which is free to access.
- Alternatively Mr Sharp could try NRT in the form of patches, chewing gum. The negatives of NRT methods are the cost of buying them and the possible side effects.

Physical activity – Mr Sharp needs to increase physical activity to reach government recommendations and to be able to play football.
- Strategies for Mr Sharp to overcome the time barrier: time – prioritise exercise in order to improve health and meet his goal. Mr Sharp could identify available time slots, e.g. straight after school, and incorporate exercise into his daily routine, whether it be walks or exercise at the gym. He could select an activity that doesn't take much time, keep sessions to a suitable duration.
- Strategies for Mr Sharp to overcome the cost barrier: he could choose activities that are free, e.g. running, walking, cycling; or he could exercise at home.
- Strategies for Mr Sharp to overcome the transport/location barrier: he could park further away from school and walk, he could use local area for walks, cycle routes.
- Strategies for Mr Sharp to overcome his lack of energy/motivation: he could schedule exercise when he has most energy, or invite a friend to join him at the gym/when training for support and motivation.

Stress – recommendations for Mr Sharp to reduce stress levels:
- Strategies for Mr Sharp are to improve his lifestyle to help alleviate stress or manage it better, e.g. more sleep, less alcohol, more exercise and a balanced diet.

Mr Sharp indicated in his screening form that on average he has 7 hours sleep per night. This is only marginally below the recommendation of 8 hours, therefore this is not a priority for Mr Sharp. However, he may find that changes to his lifestyle, including more exercise, less alcohol and a balanced diet will positively affect his sleep routine.

Diet – recommendations for Mr Sharp are to start to consume a balanced diet.
- Strategies for Mr Sharp are to utilise the Eat Well Plate for guidance on food groups and portions, to avoid skipping breakfast and to eat his evening meal earlier if possible. He needs to consider healthier alternatives to his usual foods and drink more fluids.

BMI/WHR/BP – it is recommended that Mr Sharp reduce these results, through more exercise, improvements in diet/hydration and less alcohol and smoking.

3 To complete the answer, include the following suggested points.

Mr Sharp needs to make significant changes to his current diet to work towards achieving a healthy body weight. One of the first areas for him to address is the fact that he misses breakfast on a regular basis, which is…

- **Number of meals** – breakfast is considered the 'most important meal' of the day. Mr Sharp should avoid missing this. He could consider cereal bars or fruit as an option if time is the issue.
- **Eat Well Plate** – Mr Sharp needs to refer to the Eat Well Plate particularly.
- He needs to increase his fruit/veg intake within his meals or through snacks.
- He could swap some of his current carbohydrates to brown/wholegrain options; he could increase his carbohydrate intake by eating cereal/brown toast for breakfast.
- He could incorporate more dairy through eating cereal.

- He could choose white meat/fish over red meat as they are healthier options.
- He needs to reduce food/drink high in fat, e.g. biscuits, chocolate.
- **Timing of meals** – Mr Sharp should consider eating his evening meal earlier than 7 pm, especially as he has his lunch at 12.30 pm. Again if time is an issue, this links to preparation/organisation where he could prepare healthy meals and freeze them.
- **Food choices** – Mr Sharp needs to consider swapping some food choices for healthier options, avoiding sauces such as mayonnaise or instead choosing low-fat alternatives. Where possible, Mr Sharp needs to incorporate more fruit/veg, e.g. salad in a sandwich. Crisps could be swapped for nuts, and additional fruit could be added to yoghurt to encourage Mr Sharp to achieve his 'five a day'.
- **Avoid takeaways** – Mr Sharp should consider avoiding takeaways as much as possible, as they are often high in fat. He could consider preparing similar options at home which could be much healthier.
- **Preparation/organisation** – As Mr Sharp is probably busy, being a teacher, he may find it is easier and healthier to pre-plan a menu for the week; this may avoid him straying towards a takeaway or unhealthy snacks.
- **Food labels** – when shopping, Mr Sharp should show more awareness of food labels, using them to help him choose healthier options.
- **Portion sizes** – Mr Sharp should consider his portion sizes and avoid second helpings, unless the options are healthy.
- **Fluid intake** – Mr Sharp needs to ensure he meets the target of 2-2.5 litres of fluid per day; he should consider that he may need to increase his intake when his exercise increases. He also needs to ensure that his caffeine intake does not exceed the recommended limit.

4   To complete the answer, include the following suggested points.

Mr Sharp's training aims are towards taking part in 5-a-side football in 6 weeks' time. He currently does no exercise whatsoever so training needs to start off at a low intensity. I suggest...

Mr Sharp's training methods need to focus first on achieving the government recommendations, e.g. moderate/vigorous and strength training. Once this is achieved the focus should be towards training for football.

Fartlek training is a highly suitable method of training for Mr Sharp, particularly as it can be adapted to suit football by incorporating varying intensities and changes of direction, imitating a football match. This type of training is suitable for beginners like Mr Sharp as it can incorporate low, medium and high intensity. Fartlek training can be varied by:

- Conducting training indoors and outdoors; it would be beneficial for Mr Sharp to train in a similar environment to where he will be playing football.
- **Interval training** – this involves work/rest/work periods. It can also incorporate varying. Both of these characteristics are suitable for a beginner and for football. As intensity is continually changed this can ensure boredom doesn't develop.
- **Circuit training** – can combine various areas of training, e.g. aerobic and strength, which are both areas required for Mr Sharp. Again, this type of training can be structured to the individual and the sport, e.g. as a beginner, Mr Sharp could incorporate more rest periods. Circuit training is easily adapted to avoid the boredom factor.
- **Cross training** – it is important that Mr Sharp 'cross trains' and therefore incorporates a range of training methods addressing e.g. flexibility, core, speed, within the programme.

5   To complete the answer, include the following suggested points.

Week 6 extra session – focus on improving match fitness and ability to run in short, sharp bursts required for football. It could take place in a sports hall or outdoors in a field/park.

Main activity: indoor fartlek training session
- 2 min moderate intensity (60% – 114 bpm), 2 min low intensity (50% – 95 bpm)
- 30 sec high intensity (100%), 30 sec low intensity (50% – 95 bpm) (repeat three times)
- 10 sec sprint (100%), 90 sec low intensity (50% – 95 bpm) (repeat six times)
- 30 sec high intensity (100%), 30 sec low intensity (50% – 95 bpm) (repeat three times)
- 2 min moderate intensity (60% – 114 bpm), 2 min low intensity (50% – 95 bpm)
- 10 sec sprint (100%), 90 secs low intensity (50% – 95 bpm) (repeat six times)

Cool-down: 5-min walk, reducing pace each minute.

6   To complete the answer, include the following suggested points.

Mr Sharp's training programme focuses on developing aerobic fitness in preparation for him participating in 5-a-side football. Specifically, fartlek training has been included because...

Fartlek training is a highly suitable method of training for Mr Sharp, particularly as it can be adapted to suit football by incorporating varying intensities and changes of direction, therefore imitating a football match. This type of training is suitable for beginners like Mr Sharp as it can incorporate low, medium and high intensity.

- **Frequency** – the frequency of Mr Sharp's sessions is progressive over the 6-week training programme. Weeks 1 and 2 begin with two training sessions as Mr Sharp will not have participated in exercise previous to this. In weeks 3 and 4 this is increased to three sessions per week, followed by four sessions per week in weeks 5 and 6.
- **Intensity** – the intensity of the 6 weeks will begin with levels suitable for a beginner. The heart rate training zone in week 1 is suitable for a beginner and starts off at a low intensity, e.g. 50% of Mr Sharp's MHR. Reps, sets, weight, recovery, and duration of stretches are again suitable for a beginner. In week 3 the heart rate training zone is increased to ensure that progression/overload takes place and Mr Sharp is working harder than in week 1. Within strength training the reps are increased, though sets, weight and recovery are kept the same as it is important that too many factors are not manipulated too soon. The duration of stretches is also increased to ensure development in flexibility. The intensity is also increased by adding an extra session. In week 6 the heart rate training zone is increased again to ensure progression and overload. Within strength training, reps are reduced and sets increased to 3. Again, flexibility stretches are increased in duration. Within week 6 an extra session is added, again increasing the intensity of training.
- **Time** – the duration of sessions is varied but sessions are approximately 40 mins – any longer could be too challenging and cause overtraining and injury, while too short a time would not allow a training effect to occur.
- **Type** – within the 6-week training programme, a variety of training sessions are included, e.g. aerobic, strength, flexibility, speed, all of which are suitable for training for football. Strength and flexibility exercises and circuit training focus mainly on the lower body and specifically the muscles used in football. During certain sessions a football has been introduced in some of the exercises to ensure specificity for Mr Sharp's goal of training for football. Towards the end of the training, sports-specific sessions for football are introduced to ensure Mr Sharp is 'match ready.'

- **Rest and recuperation** – as the weeks progress Mr Sharp has fewer rest days and more training; however each week he has at least two rest days to allow for growth and repair. Rest days are spaced out over the week.
- **Overload** – is incorporated within the programme. Mr Sharp overloads the body in week 1, as previous to this he has participated in no exercise. Mr Sharp continues to overload the body each week with the manipulation of the FITT principles, e.g. increasing heart rate, reps and sets, etc.
- **Progression** – over the 6 weeks, several factors are manipulated to ensure progression in training takes place.
- **Individual needs** – the programme is designed fully with Mr Sharp in mind, e.g. the fact he is new to exercise, training for football.
- **Variation** – as mentioned previously, a variety of training sessions is incorporated to avoid boredom and to ensure overload and progression in Mr Sharp's fitness.
- **Adaptation** – over the 6 weeks Mr Sharp's body will change and adapt with fitness levels increasing. It is therefore important that training sessions are modified to allow overload to continue to occur.

Revision task 2 (pages 52–70)

Reading the task information (page 52)

1 40 years old, no medical conditions so able to participate in a range of exercises, currently exercises twice a week.
2 • Works 6.00 am–2.00 pm minimum hours.
   • 45-min lunch.
   • Nurse – an active profession involving walking/lifting.
3 Very early to incorporate travel to work especially during winter months.
4 • Only 45 mins.
   • Possibly not long enough period to get changed, exercise and re-changed.
   • Possible opportunity to have a walk.
5 • Exercises twice a week at the gym.
   • Exercise needs to be appropriate for an active individual.
6 • To complete a 10 K in 6 weeks' time.

Gathering information

Making notes on lifestyle factors and screening processes (page 53)

Miss Petts: positive lifestyle factors.

Physical activity
- Exercises twice a week but still not meeting government recommendations.
- Health benefits:
  - Physical: reduces risk of chronic diseases; improves body shape; weight control.
  - Psychological: improves concentration, mood; counters depression and stress.

Smoking
- Health risks: lung-related conditions (COPD, bronchitis); heart-related (heart disease/attack, stroke); other health-related (prolonged symptoms of asthma, infertility).
- 10 health benefits to stopping smoking: breathe more easily when exercising, more energy, improved sense of smell and taste, younger looking skin.

Alcohol
- Government recommend 14 units per week.
- Short-term effects: nausea, vomiting, blackouts.
- Long-term effects: brain damage, cancers, heart attack.
- Mental health problems: stress, depression, poor sleep pattern.
- Empty calories – alcohol has no nutritional value, affects weight.

Stress
- Possible stress from nursing.
- Long-term effects: poor immune system, skin conditions, heart attack/disease, stomach ulcers.

Sleep
- Recommendation is 8 hours per night.
- Required for muscle repair, memory consolidation and release of hormones regulating growth and appetite.
- Effects of poor sleep: poor immune system, heart disease, diabetes, stress, high blood pressure.

Diet
- Eat Well Plate recommendations: plenty of fruit/veg, plenty of potatoes/bread/rice, etc, some dairy products, some meat/fish, a small amount of foods/drinks high in fat/sugar (consider whether balanced/unbalanced), eating the right amount/eating a variety of foods.
- Consider timing of meals, number of meals, food choices, alcohol intake, portion sizes, food organisation/preparation, eating slower.
- Benefits of a healthy diet: improves immune function, increases energy, prevents disease, maintains weight, improves mood.

Resting heart rate
- Factors which affect heart rate: caffeine and alcohol, exercise, disease and drugs.

	RESTING HEART RATE AGED 36–45
ATHLETE	54–59
EXCELLENT	60–64
GOOD	65–69
ABOVE AVERAGE	70–73
AVERAGE	74–78
BELOW AVERAGE	79–84
POOR	85+

BMI
- Less than 18.5 = underweight
- 18.5–24.9 = healthy weight
- 25–29.9 = overweight
- 30–39.9 = obese
- 40 or more = very obese
- Can cause health issues: high BP, diabetes

Waist-to-hip ratio
- 0.80 and below = low risk
- 0.81–0.85 = moderate risk
- 0.85+ = high risk
- Excessive weight around the waist increases risk of some diseases.

Blood pressure
- Blood pressure graph could be drawn here
- Risks associated with high BP: strain on heart and blood vessels, risk of heart attack, stroke, kidney disease, vascular dementia.

Making notes on lifestyle modification techniques (page 54)

Physical activity
- Recommendations for Miss Petts of at least 150 min of moderate activity per week.
- Or 75 min of vigorous exercise spread across the week.
- Strength training – twice a week.
- Strategies to overcome time barrier: prioritise, manage daily routine, identify available time slots, incorporate into daily routine, start a new activity, select an activity that doesn't take much time.
- Strategies to overcome the cost barrier: choose activities that are free, exercise at home.
- Strategies to overcome the transport/location barrier: park further away and walk, use local walks.

- Strategies to overcome the lack of energy/motivation: schedule exercise when she has most energy, invite a friend.

Smoking
If Miss Petts smokes recommend the following:
- Self-help tips: plan to quit, identify when she craves cigarettes and break the habit; improved diet, drinking less and exercise changes will all work in combination to reduce smoking.
- NHS smoking helpline – free support.
- NRT: e.g. patches, chewing gum – expensive and possible side effects (skin irritation, disturbed sleep, upset stomach).

Alcohol
If Miss Petts drinks above recommendation of 14 units per week:
- Self-help tips: break habit, encourage her to do something different when she would normally drink, have drink-free days, pace/space drinks, have smaller drinks.
- Reduce drinking at home: drink with food, avoid stocking up, distract herself.
- Reduce drinking while out: set a limit, opt out of rounds, budget for a fixed amount.
- External help: self-help groups, AA, drinkline, counselling, meditation, yoga.

Stress
An improved lifestyle may reduce stress levels.

Sleep
- Recommended amount: 8 hours.
- An improved lifestyle may encourage extra sleep.

Diet
- Use the Eat Well Plate to achieve a balanced diet, incorporating the right proportion and a wide variety of foods
- Consider the timing of meals.
- Number of meals.
- Food choices – consider whether she needs healthier choices for all meals/snacks.
- Consider fluid intake.
- Consider alcohol intake, consider caffeine intake.
- Better preparation and organisation of meals/snacks.

Resting heart rate
If RHR is average or below, recommend:
- less alcohol and caffeine
- more exercise.

BMI/waist-to hip ratio
If BMI/WHR is high, recommend:
- healthier eating/balanced diet
- increasing activity
- drinking more fluids.

Blood pressure
If blood pressure is high, recommend the following:
- Treatment/prevention: less salt, more fruit and veg, maintaining a healthy weight, drinking less alcohol, more exercise, stopping smoking, reducing intake of coffee, tea.

Making notes on nutritional guidance (page 55)

Eat Well Plate
- Ensure reference to the Eat Well Plate.
- Plenty of fruit/veg: incorporate through all meals/snacks.
- Plenty of potatoes, bread, rice, etc. Perhaps encourage brown or whole grain options and cereal.
- Some milk and dairy: through cereal for breakfast, yoghurts, etc.
- Some meat, fish, etc – choose white meats when possible.
- Small amounts of food/drink high in fat/sugar.

Strategies for Miss Petts
- Consider the timing of meals: does Miss Petts eat too late/early; could she eat sooner/later? Prepare meals the night before. Freeze meals to use quickly with a busy career.
- Number of meals: does Miss Petts miss any meals? If she does, she needs to be encouraged not to miss them and instead opt for a healthy option.

- Food choices (refer to her food diary) – does she need to consider healthier choices (e.g. avoid mayonnaise or choose low-fat option, incorporate salad, swap crisps for a nuts, add fruit to yoghurt)?
- Avoid takeaways, as high in fat – or prepare own fish and chips or pizza at home.
- Healthier snacks: avoid crisps, chocolate, biscuits and incorporate more fruit, cereal bars, and nuts.
- Be better prepared and organised – snacks and meals could be prepared and a menu set for the week.
- Look at food labels to check for healthier alternatives.
- Consider portion sizes.

Fluid intake
- Consider fluid intake for Miss Petts. Does she achieve the recommended 2–2.5 litres per day? May need to increase fluid when exercising.
- Water is an adequate choice of fluid.
- Caffeine needs to be in moderation. Maximum recommendation is 4–5 cups per day. It could be beneficial to reduce caffeine intake.

Making notes on training methods (page 56)

Overview
- 1st goal to increase exercise from two sessions per week and progress to achieving the government recommendations of 30 min, 5 times per week.
- Moderate/vigorous exercise for 75 min spread across the week (rather than completed in two sessions).
- Strength training – twice a week.
- 2nd goal – training towards a 10 K.
- Miss Petts – not a beginner, previous and current exercise experience.

Frequency
- Week 1: three sessions.
- Week 3: four sessions.
- Week 6: five sessions.

Intensity
- Warm-up heart rate: 40–50% (Miss Petts = 72 bpm–90 bpm).
- Target heart rate zone: 60–75% (Miss Petts = 108 bpm–135 bpm).
- Aerobic fitness zone: 70–80% (Miss Petts = 126 bpm–144 bpm).

Time
Sessions ranging from 20–60 mins.

Type
- Provide a 'cross train' for Miss Petts – a range of training methods to provide balanced conditioning, avoid boredom and injuries.
- Concentrate on 'aerobic' training for majority of sessions.
- Goal is to participate in 10 K in 6 weeks, so activities need to mimic the event and heavily include running-based activities.

Training method 1: continuous training
- Training is completed at a steady pace over a long distance.
- 20 min upwards.
- Suited for long-distance runners.

Advantages
- Effective for aerobic fitness.
- Little equipment, if any (heart rate monitor).
- Interval training.
- Work/rest/work periods.
- Changes in pace.

Training method 2: core exercises
- Holding natural running form for longer translates into improved performance.
- Reduce risk of injury.
- Flexibility training.
- A flexible body is more efficient.
- More ROM.
- Body becomes less injury prone and recovers quicker.

Miscellaneous
- Would be beneficial to incorporate other training, e.g. flexibility, core, strength, speed.
- Possibly include more components of fitness if had longer time to train (only 6 weeks available).

Making notes on designing a training programme (page 57)

Week 1: rest days – Monday, Wednesday, Friday and Sunday; training – Tuesday, Thursday and Saturday.

	Tues	Thurs	Sat
Physical activity	Outdoor run Warm-up: 5-min jog raising heart rate to 40–50% MHR (72 bpm–90 bpm). Pre-activity stretch: 10-sec (each leg) static stretches – quadriceps, hamstrings, calf (gastrocnemius/soleus), groin, gluteal, hip. Main activity – easy run: • 10-min run – 65–70% MHR (117 bpm–126 bpm) • 2-min brisk walk, recovery/hydrate (if needed). REPEAT TWICE. Developmental stretches: 15-sec stretches as above. Cool-down: 5-min walk, reducing pace and heart rate.	Gym session Warm-up: 5 min on bike, level 2 raising heart rate to 40–50% MHR (72 bpm–90 bpm). Main activity: • 10 min on rower, level 3 70–80% MHR (126 bpm–144 bpm) • 2-min rest to recover/hydrate and change machines • 10 min on cross trainer, level 3 70–80% MHR (126 bpm–144 bpm). Core/strength training: • Plank/press up/lunge (each leg) • Bicycle • All exercises – 30 sec/10 sec recovery, repeat three times. Cool-down: 5 min on bike, level 1, reducing heart rate.	Outdoor run Warm-up: 5-min jog raising heart rate to 40–50% MHR (72 bpm–90 bpm) Main activity – long run: • 40-min run 65–70% MHR (117 bpm–126 bpm) • 2-min brisk walk recovery/hydrate every 10 min (if needed) • Developmental stretches: 15-sec (each leg) static stretches – quadriceps, hamstrings, calf (gastrocnemius/soleus), groin, gluteal, hip. Cool-down: 5-min walk, reducing pace and heart rate.

Week 3: rest days – Monday, Wednesday and Friday; training – Tuesday, Thursday, Saturday and Sunday.

Warm-ups/cool-downs/pre-activity stretches/development stretches as per week 1 unless otherwise specified.

	Tues	Thurs	Sat	Sun
Physical activity	Outdoor run As per week 1 (Tues) – increase duration to 15 min.	(Additional session) Outdoor run Warm-up: 5-min jog raising heart rate to 40–50% MHR (72 bpm–90 bpm). Pre-activity stretch: as per week 1 (Tues). Main activity – progressive run: • 10-min run – 65–70% MHR (117 bpm–126 bpm) • 10-min run – 70%–75% (126 bpm–135 bpm) • 10-min run – 75%–80% (135 bpm–144 bpm) • 2-min brisk walk, recovery/hydrate every 10 min (if needed). Resistance band stretches (two sets of 8 reps, 30-sec recovery): sit to stand/core twist/squat/side leg raises/arm swing. Cool-down: 5-min walk, reducing pace and heart rate.	Gym session As per week 1 (Thurs) – increase duration of rower/cross trainer to 15 min. Core/strength training: same exercises – increase duration to 45 sec.	Outdoor run As per week 1 (Sat) – increase duration to 50-min run. Developmental stretches: as per week 1 – increase stretch to 20 sec (each leg).

Week 6: rest days – Monday and Friday; training – Tuesday, Wednesday, Thursday and Saturday; 10 K race: Sunday.

Warm-ups/cool-downs/pre-activity stretches/development stretches: as per week 3 unless otherwise specified.

	Tues	Wed	Thurs	Sat
Physical activity	Progressive run as per week 3 (Thurs).	Easy run as per week 3 (Tues).	Gym session as per week 3 (Sat).	20-min recovery jog. Activity recovery zone for heart rate – 60% of MHR (108 bpm).

Making notes on justifying your training programme (page 59)

- All sessions have a warm-up, main activity and cool-down.

Frequency
- Weeks 1/2: three sessions – progressed for current two sessions.
- Week 3/4: four sessions.
- Week 5/6: five training sessions, including the 10 K race.
- **Progressed** frequency – gradually to avoid overtraining, injury.

Intensity

Aerobic training
- Runs – outdoor to mimic 10 K.
- Warm-up to allow heart rate to increase gradually.
- Cool-down to allow heart rate to decrease gradually.
- Runs to incorporate recovery periods if required.
- **Progression of aerobic** – duration of runs to increase week 3/6.
- Increase heart rate training zone to ensure she works harder.
- Frequency of runs to increase as sessions/weeks progress.
- Combination of easy/hard run to challenge, add variation.

Gym session
- To allow for cross training – still developing aerobic fitness but not overtraining via running.
- **Progression of aerobic** – increase duration of activities.
- Increase heart rate training zone to ensure she works harder.

Core exercises
- To boost posture/improve technique for running.
- **Progression of core** – increase duration of exercises.

Flexibility
- Pre-activity stretches to prepare the muscles for running.
- Developmental stretches, incorporated at the end to help develop flexibility in muscles used in running, will improve performance.
- **Progression of flexibility** – increase duration of stretches.

Time
- Sessions lasting 40 min +.
- 20-min + aerobic training is an acceptable/optimal timeframe.
- Not all cardio in this time – mixture of strength and flexibility/core.

Type
- Training sessions – **variation** of aerobic, strength, flexibility, and core – all required for a runner.
- Cross training to ensure balanced conditioning, avoid boredom and injuries.
- Continuous training to mimic 10 K.
- Flexibility **specifically** concentrating on lower body – muscles required for a runner.
- Static stretching.
- Resistance band stretches – ensure progression in flexibility, to ensure balanced conditioning, avoid boredom and injuries.
- Strength **specifically** concentrating on lower body and core muscles required for a runner, improve running and toning legs, bum and tum.

Principles of training
- **Rest and recuperation** – rest days, which reduce as training progresses, allow for growth and repair.
- **Overload** – ensuring Miss Petts is working above what she is used to: definitely in week 1 as activity increases in frequency, continue to overload by changing FITT principles.
- **Progression** – in activities over the 6 weeks, factors are manipulated to ensure progression – reps, sets, heart rate, time, training types.
- **Individual needs** – planned specifically to match Miss Petts' aim/level of fitness and sport.
- **Variation** – mixture of outdoor and indoor sessions, variety of training sessions to avoid boredom and to ensure overload and greater progress.
- **Adaptation** – actions will become easier and body will adapt.

Preparation before the 10 K
- Weeks 4/5 – you would expect to see progression in training at its highest.

Week 6: light sessions while preparing for 10 K
- Reduce training duration.
- Day before – recovery jog to aid recovery, remove waste.

Reviewing additional information (pages 60–63)
Current activity levels (page 60)

1 Already active twice a week, looking to gradually increase frequency. Week 1 could start with one additional session.

Nutritional status (page 61)

1 Limited fruit and vegetables, food choices high in fat/sugar (e.g. crisps/chocolate/takeaway), not achieving recommended hydration levels, alcohol intake could be above recommendations (if continued) for rest of week. Porridge good source of slow-release carbohydrate.

2 Food choices high in fat/sugar (e.g. crisps/biscuits/cheese/takeaway), not achieving recommended hydration levels, alcohol intake higher than day 1 and could be above recommendations (if continued) for rest of week. Porridge good source of slow-release carbohydrate. Some vegetables through salad, limited fruit.

Physical activity/sporting goals (page 63)

1 • 15 units is slightly above government recommendations for alcohol intake per week.
   • This will negatively affect the body (short- and long-term effects) and training.
2 • Classified as overweight in relation to her height and weight.
   • This will negatively affect the body and training.

Questions (page 64)

1 To complete the answer, include the following suggested points.

   Negative factor – **physical exercise** – does not complete enough physical exercise.
   • Below government recommendations for physical activity based on her age.
   • Negative effects on health and well-being of lack of exercise, e.g. physical/psychological.
   • More exercise may reduce Miss Petts' weight/BMI/WHR and help her sleep more.

   Negative factor – **unbalanced diet** – limited food groups/limited hydration/eating takeaways/too much alcohol and caffeine/timing of meals/poor snack choices, etc.
   • Not achieving government recommendations/guidelines for diet.
   • Negative effects on health and well-being of an unbalanced diet, e.g. poor immune system, weight increase, impairs mood.
   • An improved diet may reduce Miss Petts' weight/BMI/WHR.

   Negative factor – **alcohol consumption** – drinks 15 units per week.
   • Exceeds government recommendations for alcohol consumption which is 14 units.
   • Negative effects of alcohol, e.g. short-/long-term effects/mental health problems.
   • Less alcohol may reduce Miss Petts' weight/BMI/WHR, help her sleep more, and may reduce number of cigarettes smoked as may be consumed together.

   Negative factor – **smoking** – 5 per day.
   • Negative effects of smoking, e.g. lung-, heart- and other health-related conditions.
   • Quitting smoking may allow Miss Petts to breathe more easily when running.

   Negative factor – **lack of sleep** – 6 hours per day.
   • Negative effects of lack of sleep, e.g. stress/high blood pressure.
   • More sleep may increase Miss Petts' motivation to exercise.

   Positive factor – that she participates in some exercise already, no stress.

Positive factor – **resting heart rate** – classified as average.

Positive factor – **blood pressure** – classified as average.

Negative factor – **BMI** – classified as overweight.

- Risks associated with high BMI, e.g. hypertension, cardiovascular disease, diabetes.
- Increased exercise/improved diet/less alcohol will improve BMI.

Negative factor – **waist to-hip ratio** – classified as moderate risk.

- Risks associated with high WHR, e.g. increased risk of certain diseases.
- Increased exercise/improved diet/less alcohol will improve WHR.

2 To complete the answer, include the following suggested points.

Physical activity – Miss Petts needs to increase physical activity to reach government recommendations and to train towards a 10 K.

- Strategies for Miss Petts to overcome the **time** barrier: she could prioritise exercise in order to improve health and meet her goal. Miss Petts could identify available time slots, e.g. straight after work, and incorporate exercise into her daily routine, whether it be runs home or going to the gym.
- Strategies for Miss Petts to overcome the **cost** barrier: she already has access to gym facilities, but if cost is an issue she could choose activities which are free, e.g. running, walking, cycling or she could exercise at home.
- Strategies for Miss Petts to overcome the **transport/location** barrier: she could park further away from work and walk. She could use local area for walks, cycle routes. She could run/cycle to work.
- Strategies for Miss Petts to overcome the **lack of energy/motivation barrier**: she could schedule exercise when she has most energy, e.g. straight after work. She could invite a friend to join her at the gym/training for support and motivation.

Smoking – recommend that Miss Petts gives up smoking.

- Strategies for Miss Petts to quit: start with self-help tips, as well as an improvement in diet/drinking/exercise, which may mean she naturally stops smoking or smokes less.
- If the above methods are ineffective she could try the NHS stop-smoking service, which is free to access.
- She could try NRT in the form of patches, chewing gum. The negatives of NRT methods are the cost of buying them and their possible side effects.

Alcohol – recommend that Miss Petts reduce alcohol intake first to within the government recommendations, and then further to be able to lose weight, be healthier and more able to train effectively.

- Strategies for Miss Petts to reduce alcohol intake: start with self-help tips, as well as an improvement in diet/exercise/smoking, which may mean she naturally stops drinking as much.
- Strategies for Miss Petts to reduce alcohol at home: drink with food, avoid stocking up with alcohol, keep distracted.
- Strategies for Miss Petts to reduce alcohol while out: set a drinking limit, opt out of rounds and budget a fixed amount to spend on drinking.
- If the above methods are ineffective and her drinking becomes an issue, she could try external help, but at this stage this is not necessary.

Sleep – recommend that Miss Petts get more sleep.

- Strategies to help Miss Petts improve her sleep are to improve her lifestyle: less alcohol, more exercise and a balanced diet. Also a regular bedtime routine.

Diet – recommend that Miss Petts start to consume a balanced diet.

- Strategies for Miss Petts to start to consume a balanced diet: utilise the Eat Well Plate for guidance on food groups and portions, consider the timing of her meals, opt for healthier alternatives and drink more fluids.

BMI/WHR – recommendation is to reduce these results through more exercise, improvements in diet/hydration and less alcohol.

3 To complete the answer, include the following suggested points.

Eat Well Plate – Miss Petts needs to refer to the Eat Well Plate, particularly:

- She needs to increase her fruit/veg intake within her meals or through snacks.
- She could swap/reduce some of her current carbohydrates to brown/wholegrain options.
- She could incorporate more dairy through eating e.g. yoghurts; these could also combine fruit.
- She could choose white meat/fish over red meat as they are healthier options.
- She needs to reduce food/drink high in fat, e.g. biscuits, chocolate.

Number of meals/timing of meals – Miss Petts eats a nutritional breakfast of porridge; this could be combined with some fruit. Miss Petts eats breakfast, lunch and dinner; however the lunch and dinner choices are not as nutritional. Miss Petts should consider eating her lunch later (if possible) as there is a huge gap in time between lunch and dinner, which may mean she snacks. If she does snack these need to be healthy choices. Again, if time is an issue, this links to preparation/organisation in that she could prepare healthy meals and freeze them.

Food choices – Miss Petts needs to consider swapping some food choices for healthier options, e.g. less cheese on sandwiches, opting for salad instead of sandwiches. Where possible, Miss Petts needs to incorporate more fruit/veg, whether it be within a meal or as a snack. Crisps could be swapped for nuts and yoghurt for chocolate, with additional fruit added to the yoghurt to encourage Miss Petts to achieve her 'five a day'.

Avoid takeaways – Miss Petts should consider avoiding takeaways as much as possible, as they are often high in fat. She could consider preparing similar options at home which could be much healthier.

Preparation/organisation – as Miss Petts is probably busy as a nurse, she may find it is easier and healthier to pre-plan a menu for the week; this may avoid her straying towards a takeaway or unhealthy snacks.

Food labels – when shopping, Miss Petts should show more awareness of food labels, using them to help her choose healthier options.

Portion sizes – Miss Petts should consider her portion sizes and avoid second helpings, unless the options are healthy.

Fluid intake – Miss Petts needs to work towards consuming more fluid throughout her day; she could take a water bottle to work to keep on hand. She needs to reduce her caffeine intake and limit herself to fewer than four cups of coffee per day. The same applies for sugary drinks, which need to be reduced.

4 To complete the answer, include the following suggested points.

Miss Petts' training methods need to focus first on achieving the government recommendations, e.g. moderate/vigorous and strength training; once this is achieved the focus should be towards training for her 10 K, so the majority of training will be focused on developing aerobic fitness and running-based activities.

Continuous training – is an effective training method for improving aerobic fitness. It involves training at a steady pace over distance, which mimics the 10 K that Miss Petts is training towards. Continuous training can be varied by adapting the route, distance, terrain, pace, etc. This will avoid Miss Petts becoming bored with her training. This type of training can be conducted indoors and outdoors, so training doesn't have to be affected by the weather. It would be beneficial for Miss Petts to train on a similar terrain to where she will complete her 10 K.

Interval training – this involves work/rest/work periods, and can be used when running to develop aerobic fitness. Again, as intensity is continually changed this can ensure boredom doesn't develop. This training can be conducted indoors and outdoors.

Cross training – it is important that Miss Petts 'cross trains', and therefore incorporates a range of training methods, e.g. continuous, interval, core and flexibility, to enable balanced conditioning and avoid boredom and injuries.

5 To complete the answer, include the following suggested points.
   Week 1: rest days – Monday, Wednesday, Friday and Sunday; training – Tuesday, Thursday and Saturday.

	Tuesday	Thursday	Saturday
Physical activity	**Outdoor run** **Warm-up:** 5-min jog raising heart rate to 40–50% MHR (72 bpm–90 bpm) **Pre-activity stretch:** 10-sec (each leg) static stretches: quadriceps, hamstrings, calf (gastrocnemius/ soleus), groin, gluteal, hip **Main activity:** Easy run 10-min run – 65–70% MHR (117 bpm–126 bpm) 2-min brisk walk recovery/hydrate (if needed) REPEAT TWICE **Developmental stretches:** 15-sec, as above **Cool-down:** 5-min walk, reducing pace and heart rate.	**Gym session** **Warm-up:** 5-min on bike, level 2, raising heart rate to 40–50% MHR (72 bpm–90 bpm) **Main activity:** 10 min on rower, level 3, 70–80% MHR (126 bpm–144 bpm) 2-min rest to recover/hydrate and change machines 10 min on cross trainer, level 3, 70–80% MHR (126 bpm–144 bpm) **Core/strength training:** Plank/press up/lunge (each leg) Bicycle All exercises – 30 sec/10-sec recovery, repeat 3 times **Cool-down:** 5-min on bike, level 1, reducing heart rate.	**Outdoor run** **Warm-up :** 5-min jog raising heart rate to 40–50% MHR (72 bpm–90 bpm) **Main activity:** Long run 40-min run, 65–70% MHR, (117 bpm–126 bpm) 2-min brisk walk recovery/hydrate every 10 mins (if needed) **Developmental stretches:** 15-sec (each leg) static stretches: quadriceps, hamstrings, calf (gastrocnemius/soleus), groin, gluteal, hip **Cool-down:** 5-min walk, reducing pace and heart rate.

Week 3: rest days – Monday, Wednesday and Friday; training – Tuesday, Thursday, Saturday and Sunday.
Warm-ups/cool-downs/pre-activity stretches/development stretches: as per week 1, unless otherwise specified.

	Tuesday	Thursday	Saturday	Sunday
Physical activity	**Outdoor run** As per week 1 (Tues), increase duration to 15 min.	**(Additional session) Outdoor run** **Warm-up:** 5-min jog raising heart rate to 40–50% MHR (72 bpm –90 bpm) **Pre–activity stretch:** as per week 1 (Tues) **Main activity: progressive run** 10-min run – 65–70% MHR, (117 bpm–126 bpm) 10-min run – 70%–75% MHR (126 bpm–135 bpm) 10-min run – 75%–80% MHR (135 bpm–144 bpm) 2-min brisk walk recovery/hydrate every 10 mins (if needed) **Resistance band stretches**: 2 sets of 8 reps, 30-sec recovery: sit to stand/core twist/squat/side leg raises/arm swing **Cool-down:** 5-min walk, reducing pace and heart rate.	**Gym session** As per week 1 (Thurs), increase duration of rower/cross trainer to 15 min. **Core/strength training:** Same exercises, increase duration to 45 sec.	**Outdoor run** As per week 1 (Sat), increase duration to 50-min run **Developmental stretches:** as per week 1, increase stretch duration to 20 sec (each leg).

Week 6: rest days – Monday and Friday; training – Tuesday, Wednesday, Thursday and Saturday; 10 K race: Sunday.
Warm-ups/cool-downs/pre-activity stretches/development stretches: as per week 3, unless otherwise specified.

	Tuesday	Wednesday	Thursday	Saturday
Physical activity	**Progressive run** as per week 3 (Thurs).	**Easy run** as per week 3 (Tues).	**Gym session** as per week 3 (Sat).	20-min recovery jog Activity recovery zone for heart rate – 60% of MHR, (108 bpm).

6 To complete the answer, include the following suggested points.

Frequency – the frequency of the sessions is progressive. Weeks 1/2 begin with three training sessions, weeks 3/4 increase to four sessions, weeks 5/6 increase to five sessions. The frequency is planned to progress slowly as it is important for the sessions not to be so challenging that Miss Petts can't manage them and also to avoid overtraining and injury.

Intensity – the intensity of the 6 weeks will begin with levels suitable for Miss Petts, who already trains twice a week. The heart rate training zone in week 1 is suitable for Miss Petts getting back into running training specifically. Recovery periods are incorporated to avoid the training being too challenging too soon; these recovery periods will reduce over the 6 weeks as fitness improves. Over the 6-week period the frequency and duration of training sessions is to increase, so heart rate will gradually be increased to achieve a maximum of 70–80% in order to develop aerobic fitness as much as possible. Within Miss Petts' training week there will be a combination of easy/hard runs, in order to provide a challenge, allow recovery and avoid boredom. Core stability and flexibility are important components when running, therefore they feature in Miss Petts' training programme, to boost her posture/ROM, and ultimately to improve her running technique, as well as to avoid injury. The duration of these exercises will be manipulated to ensure progression and overload. With flexibility training, pre-activity exercises have been included to fully prepare the muscles for running; these are then followed at the end of the session with developmental stretches, focusing on developing flexibility of the muscles used within running.

Time – the duration of sessions varies and progresses but sessions are approximately 40 min plus. Again, much longer could be too challenging and cause overtraining and injury, while too short a time would not allow for an aerobic training effect to occur – anything above 20 mins is required for aerobic fitness. Sessions are not all cardio within the time, but also a combination of strength/core and flexibility.

Type – within the 6-week training programme, a variety of training sessions is included, e.g. aerobic, strength, flexibility, core, all of which are required for running. Strength and flexibility exercises focus mainly on the lower body and specifically the muscles used in running. The majority of training is aerobic and running-based to ensure specificity for Miss Petts' goal of training for a 10K. However, the gym session incorporates a range of cardiovascular machines to allow Miss Petts a rest from too much running, while still focusing on developing aerobic fitness. In particular, continuous training outdoors is used, as this closely mimics a 10K race.

Rest and recuperation – as the weeks progress, Miss Petts has fewer rest days and more training; however, each week she has at least two rest days to allow for growth and repair. Rest days are spaced out over the week.

Overload – is incorporated within the programme. Miss Petts overloads the body in week 1, as an extra session is added and her previous gym sessions are modified. Miss Petts continues to overload the body each week with the manipulation of the FITT principles, e.g. increasing heart rate, distance.

Progression – over the 6 weeks, several factors are manipulated to ensure progression in training takes place.

Individual needs – the programme is designed fully with Miss Petts in mind, in particular taking into consideration the 10K she is going to run.

Variation – as mentioned previously, a variety of training sessions is incorporated to avoid boredom and to ensure overload and progression in Miss Petts' fitness.

Adaptation – over the 6 weeks, Miss Petts' body will change and adapt with fitness levels increasing, therefore it is important that training sessions are modified so that overload continues to occur.

Preparation before the 10K – during weeks 4 and 5, training will be at its most intense for Miss Petts. Week 6 will be a light week of training in preparation for the 10K, so the duration of training and heart rate is reduced and the final session is focused on recovery and removing waste before the race.